MW01630135

THE GREAT TEMPLE
OF MADURAI MEENAKSHI

Thiruppugazh amudhan
VALAYAPETTAI RA. KRISHNAN

PUBLISHED BY

ARULMIGU MEENAKSHI SUNDARESHWARAR TEMPLE
MADURAI

All rights are reserved. No part of this publication may be transmitted or reproduced in any form or by any means without prior permission from the publisher.

First Edition   - November 2014
Second Edition - March 2015

Copyright ©2014
ISBN: 978-88-1920700-1-8

THE GREAT TEMPLE
OF MADURAI MEENAKSHI

Author : Valayapettai Ra. Krishnan
Editing : Dr. R. Mahadevan
Photography : Vamsi Krishna, D. Chandrasekar, S. Jagannathan, M.A. Sekhar, R. Prasad
Translation : S. Sivakumar
Creative : P. Venkatareddy
Colour Illustration : M.A. Shankar Lingam
Design : GD. Karthik, KSP. Reddy

Published by
Joint Commissioner / Executive Officer,
Arulmighu Meenakshi Sundareswarar Temple,
Madurai 625 001.Tamil Nadu.
Telephone 091- 452- 2344360.
Fax 091- 452- 2341777
Email mmtemplejc@gmail.com
Website : www.maduraimeenakshi.org

In Association with

Universal Publishing
69, Royapettah High Road,
142 IOA Complex,
Chennai - 600 014. INDIA.
Tel: 9840789096

Cover Design : View of South Gopuram

Preface

MADURAI - the name at once evokes a feeling of devotion and awe; devotion towards Mother Meenakshi and Lord Sundareshwarar, the presiding deities at the most famous Madurai Meenakshi Temple of Tamil Nadu and awe at the long, uninterrupted history of literature, art and architecture that flourished in this temple town from pre-Christian era to the present day. That the divine grace and compassion of Goddess Meenakshi pervades and permeates through every aspect of life in this region, can be the only reason that through several changes of dynastic rules, wars and vicissitudes, Madurai has been the centre of attraction for thousands of years to pilgrims and tourists, traders and travelers, Kings and commoners from all over the world.

Apart from being a place of religious worship for centuries, held sacred by generations of Hindus, the architecture and design of the temple complex, the *mandapams* and the sculptures therein, the paintings and festivals, all combine to make the temple a visitor's paradise. Anonymous sculptors and artists have lavished their masterly skills in embellishing the tall and majestic towers and the pillared halls in and around the sanctum, adding a stunning beauty to their sheer size and massiveness.

The historic events that shaped the city under different rulers and the myriad legends around the deities are beautifully captured in the brilliant art forms one can see in the Meenakshi temple. A discerning observer can piece together how generations of kings vied with one another in adding luster to the abode of their guardian deity, by constructing a corridor here and a mandapam there, adding an arch here and a few sculptures there.

The temple on the whole is a treasure house depicting the evolution of art and architecture of South India and the magnificent heights they were able to reach under the rule of Pandiyars and Nayakars. A casual visitor will be struck with wonder and amazement at the majesty and grandeur of the towers and the multitude of sculptures, but a discerning enthusiast would like to understand and appreciate the story that the stones tell. This book is intended to provide a guide for such an experience.

In bringing out this book, the immense co-operation and assistance from Shri. Karumuttu T. Kannan, Fit Person and Shri. P. Dhanapal, Commissioner HR&CE and Administration of the Arulmigu Meenakshi Sundareswarar Temple. The involvement and the helpful interest from the staff and officers of HR&CE Department is gratefully acknowledged.

My sincere thanks to Sri. S.Sivakumar for the lucid translation, Dr.R.Mahadhaven for the fine editing job with dedication and Shri J.Lakshmi Narayanan for his creative and total involvement in this production.

I belive that is book will occupy a pride of place in every lover of Tamil Nadu temples and connoisseur of the art and architecture of such Indian temples as well as devotees of Goddess Meenakshi.

Valayapettai Ra. Krishnan

Contents

Evolution of South Indian Temples

The fertile lands of the Indian Subcontinent have seen the birth of many religions and philosophies, of which, the earliest and greatest contribution is Hinduism. Often described as a 'way of life', Hinduism integrated into itself several beliefs and concepts from other contemporary faiths, including those of its early adversaries. However, it managed to retain its core principles and central philosophy which endures even to this day. The origin of Hinduism goes so far back that it is difficult to be definite about a specific date. It is however a well known fact that India was the cradle of one of the most ancient civilizations. At some point in the continuing development of this civilization, man, from being a hunter and gatherer of food to meet his physical needs, realized the presence of an omnipotent force- a force, he saw manifested in the elements of nature. He could experience it in the soil he worked on, the Sun above, the blowing wind, the falling rain, the stars of the night sky and in space. This experience soon transformed into faith and in time, to worship. Starting from simple acts of devotion to Mother Nature, it evolved into personification of Natural forces into symbols and eventually to idols. The connection with Nature was still retained, as these deities were worshipped under the shade of large trees, hill tops, caves and in other natural environs.

The plains of South India saw the manifestation of this belief in worship, develop in a more forceful and demonstrative fashion. Human creativity was harnessed by a long line of supportive Kings and Queens, to build massive edifices in the form of lofty temples. With the guidance of religious preceptors and involvement of artists and architects, innumerable temples came up across the length and breadth of South India - to such an extent that a village without a temple was considered unfit for human habitation.

Shore Temple Complex at Mamallapuram built during the reign of Narasimhavarman II (700-778 AD) of Pallava Dynasty

Early medieval Chola Temple, Narthamalai, TN

Stone inscription during Pallava Dynasty

Pre-History

As we get closer to recorded history, the earliest in South India belonging to the 3rd Century BC, we find surprisingly a very few standing temples or even dated ruins of this period. Though the *Sangam* works (the earliest confluence of Tamil scholars) have pointed references to worship, their dates are still being debated. Realizing that until the early half of the 7th Century AD, there are possibly very few temples whose remains have been comprehensively dated. Scholars propose the theory that early temples were fashioned out of perishable materials. There is clearly a need to study the pre-recorded period in greater depth.

Birth of the Sthala Vruksham

The *Sangam* period was considered the golden age of Tamil Nadu as it was the period of exciting evolution in every sphere whether it was art, literature, poetry or human progress. On the one hand the people of Tamil Nadu moved towards more formal structures for temples and on the other hand the concept of *Sthala Vruksham*. These were generally trees which had abundant medicinal properties like the Neem, Peepul, Banyan, Fig, Bael, Jamun, Gooseberry and Pomegranate. The *Sthala Vruksham* of Madurai is the *Kadamba* Tree. A legend states that Lord Sundareshwara was discovered by Lord Indra under a *Kadamba* Tree.

In some places, the names of the trees became the name of the God or the name of the village. Tiruvaalangadu, Tiruverkadu, Tirukachi Ekambam (Kanchipuram), Tiruvidaimarudur, Tirupanandal, Tiruppathirippuliyur are some examples for the above. There is even a place called "Tirukallil" named after the *Kalli* plant (Cactus) under which God was worshipped.

The Art of Temple Building

The origins of formal temple worship could be traced to the worship of *Shiva Lingams* in dense forests and places of natural beauty. Legends attributed these *Lingams* to *Swayambhu* (appeared on their own) and it was believed that celestial beings worshipped them at nights while human beings worshipped during day.

With the progress of civilization, devotees wanted to protect their idols which had been left in the open, against the vagaries of nature and wild animals. Initially, they surrounded the *Lingam* with a fence made of wood from the forest. The height was not much but it acted as a protective barrier for the idol. The concept of "*Garbhagriha*" (Sanctum Sanctorum)was thus born and the first temples made of wood were built.

With the march of civilization, the wooden temples evolved into temples made of mud. During the *Sangam* period, the wooden structures were surrounded by structures made of mud and a roof was built to protect the idol from the sun and rain. During the fifth century A.D, the practice of building temples with bricks came into existence. Today, these ancient temples made of mud or bricks do not exist in Tamil Nadu, but are present in Kerala.

The next trend was that people started to migrate and build their homes around these structures. Villages and towns flourished around these temples which became the centre of their activities.

The Sangam Style

Ancient Tamil texts like *Thevaram* and *Perumpanatruppadai* throw light on the kind of temples of that time and there is a reference to *Sudumann* and *Mann thali*. The former might mean

Kailasanath Temple, Kanchipuram, built by Pallavas in the early 8th Century AD

the brick structures and the latter may denote the mud temples. The *Thevaram* of Sri Tirunavukkarasar has elaborate descriptions of temples which existed in the sixth century AD and before. Tirunavukkarasar speaks of eight types of temples namely *Perunkoil, Maadakkoil, Karakkoil, Gnazhar Koil, Kokudikkoil, Ilankoil, Manikkoil* and *Aalakkoil* which existed in his time.

The Chola King Kochenganan who lived towards the end of the *Sangam* period constructed seventy *Maadakkoils*. The salient feature of these *Maadakkoils* was that the sanctum sanctorum used to be on a higher plane. Such temples made of stone are found at Aakkur, Kizhvelur, Vaihal and Saikkadu. Though the structure of each of these temples varied, their objective remained the same- worship.

Pride of the Pallavas

The evolutionary development theory substantiates the claim of Mahendra Pallava during 630 AD, where he proudly proclaimed his role in bringing to permanence the abode of the gods – stone sculpture introducing.

The Pallavas have bequeathed for posterity their magnificent rock cut temples. The Pallavas ruled over Tamil Nadu for over 300 years from the sixth century AD, with Kanchipuram as their headquarters. They initiated a sea change in the construction of temples. They viewed temples more as an art form and their temples were stunning galleries showcasing intricate pieces of art. In fact, they were the pioneers of sculpture in design of temples.

The Pallavas realised that the temples made of bricks or wood would not stand the test of time and would succumb to nature. They identified black stone as the most durable material for their creations. The abundance of natural caves and those created in natural rocks became their choice. They transformed these caves into magnificent temples by crafting sculptures and installing the deities there.

Within a short span of time, the brilliant creative genius of Pallava clan, manifested through Mahendra, Mamalla and their great grandson Rajasimhan, who sidestepped slow evolutionary growth, leaping over a large chasm in experimenting with stone. Excavating rock cut temples, monolithic *rathas* and magnificent bas reliefs, they understood the difficulties in such an exercise and quickly leap frogged into working on structural temples.

Eigth Century AD was the brightest for the art of the Pallavas during the reign of Rajasimha, for he initiated exemplary structures to be built, starting with the Shore Temples at Mamallapuram on to the Vaikunta Perumal Temple before celebrating the beauty of artistic expression in the Kailasanathar Temple at Kanchipuram.

A sea change was beginning to occur in the concept of the deities as well, for, the *Agamas* started to crystalise. As temples grew more opulent, the main deities became larger and the need for a processional deity arose. The period saw the fashioning of some very early images of Gods and Goddesses cast in bronze.

Big Temple at Thanjavur built by Cholas in the 11th Century

The Rise of the Gopuram and Vimanam

In the continuing evolution of temples, the construction of the *Gopuram* and *Vimanam* became the next trend. As the practice of religious worship spread far and wide, so did the artistic sense and *Gopuram* construction which became an inseparable part of the temple. The lofty towers seemed to reflect the opulence and devotion of the benefactor, often fuelled by a healthy competition among the temples.

Charm of the Cholas

The construction of stone temples continued during the eighth century AD for about 250 years in the reign of the Cholas. Many temples whose structure was originally made of bricks were now reconstructed with stone under the illustrious Queen Chembian Maadevi. The Emperor Raja Raja took the concept of temples to their glorious height as he envisioned the *Vimana* as the Mount Meru itself and forever enshrined his name with that of his masterpiece - the Brahadiswara Temple at Thanjavur in 1010 AD. His reign also saw the art of Bronze-casting reach hitherto unexplored heights, as the Emperor's personal fondness to Shiva and his dancing form, saw the genesis of the Nataraja image. His son Rajendra Chola embarked on a similar task to erect the equally massive yet stylistically differing Gangaikonda Cholapuram Temple at Gangai Konda Cholapuram around 1025 AD. Following these temples, the same style was adopted in many temples like the Darasuram Iravatheswar Temple near Kumbakonam and the Kampahareswar temple at Tribhuvanam.

The reign of the Cholas in the initial period of the ninth century, was one of the best periods for the development of temple architecture. This was the period when the development of sculptures from stone also reached its zenith. The Cholas also started gaining name and fame for building huge temples.

The Pandyas Elevate Dravidian Architecture

The Pandyas during the reign of Maravarman Sundara Pandya (1218 AD) broke free from Chola dominance and Madurai worked over time to return to the peak of its glory. In a short span of just under 100 years, Dravidian architecture also rose to equally great heights. The Pandyas cleverly added new dimensions and nuances that brought more grandeur to the temple structures.

The Cholas kept the intricate and beautiful designs of architecture restricted to the Sanctum Sanctorum and its *Vimana*. However, the Pandya kings extended these intricate designs to the other parts of the temple and also extended the temple area by building many *mandapams* around the sanctum sanctorum and also high walls to fortify the temple. They also built *Gopurams* at the entrances in the walls. The tall *Gopurams* which beautify the temples as we see today were first built by the Pandya kings. They also created ponds with lotus flowers inside the temples.

The architecture of the Pandya period is commented upon by Percy Brown thus, "Pandian period is a period of transition between the affluent maturity of the Cholas and the exquisite, though extravagant production of Vijayanagar."

The Epicentre of Art and Literature

Generally Hindu temples went beyond their function of worship and served as a place to showcase human talent. Each one is like a gallery of sculptures, the *Vimanam*, the *Mandapam* and the *Gopuram*, with sculptures depicting scenes from our *Puranas* and legends. In addition to these were the sculptures cast in copper and bronze. Sculpting in metals became a speciality of Tamilnadu.

Temples also served as schools as well as courts which rendered justice. The society participated with a great deal of enthusiasm and considered it their duty and right to undertake various tasks in organising Temple festivals. Thus temples and the society became inseparable. Various forms of literature like *Kalambakams, Pillai Thamizh, Thoodhu* and *Ula* were composed by many poets and the temple served as a platform to showcase their works. In addition to these forms, the practice of daily reading of the epics of the Ramayana and the Mahabharata in the temples was also prevalent. There was also the practice of gifting lands to the people who recite these sacred hymns in the temples for the benefit of the public.

As Sri Aurobindo said, "A great oriental work of art does not easily reveal its secret to one who comes to it solely in a mood of aesthetic curiosity or with a critical objective mind..... it has to be seen in loneliness; in the solitude of one's self in moments when one is capable of long and deep meditation." That would take a lot of effort and the task can be made easy by a helpful guide that provides the necessary insights for such an understanding and appreciation.

Gangaikonda Choleeswaram constructed by Rajendra Chola I during 11th Century AD

Madurai - its Legacy and Legends

Madurai through the ages

The very utterance of the word Madurai ushers in the legends of yore, of the two earlier sites of the famed capital of the Pandyan kings which were submerged by the sea, along with an enormous corpus of lost Tamil literature, forcing the shift of the capital to interior parts of the land. The surviving *Sangam* works, refer to the sacred land as "Madurai" but more often as *"Koodal"* or even *"Naanmaada Koodal", "Koodal Nagar", "Thiruaalavai"* or simply *"Aalavai"*.

Koodal could just refer to a meeting point, but the richness of the word actually implies a confluence. It could have meant the confluence of the river with the ocean and the same name, to denote the earlier location near the sea might have been retained for the new venue. Another possibility is that it referred to the confluence of scholars as they assembled in the famous *Sangam*, where poets would arrive, stay together and involve themselves in debate and research.

Madurai was known by other names which testify to the great sanctity of the *kshethram* (Holy Place).

Madurai was once covered with *Kadamba* forests which were cleared by Kulasekara Pandyan before the City was built on well planned lines. Hence the city was called 'Kadambavana kshethram'. The *Thiruvilayadal Puranam* (Divine Sport) states that after a deluge, Lord Sundareshwarar sent a serpant to point out to the Pandya king the boundaries of the original City of Madurai as it had existed before the deluge. So the City came to be known as *Aalavai* or *Thiru Alavai* in Tamil.

The *Thevaram* verses are full of praise for the Lord of the City and address him as *Aalavai Annal*. The exact meaning of the ancient word Aalavai is lost over the ages. In its current form Madurai is said to be derived from *Madhu* in Tamil, meaning the sweet nectar contained in flowers. There is a legend for it too - that when the beautiful city was built, Lord Shiva himself came to bless and a drop of nectar from his locks fell on the city, giving it its beautiful name.

References to Madurai abound in the literary works with the earliest being the account of Megasthenes in the 3rd Century BC, when he refers to the city as "Methora" and also in *Kautilya's Arthashastra*.

Artistic Impression of Ancient Madurai

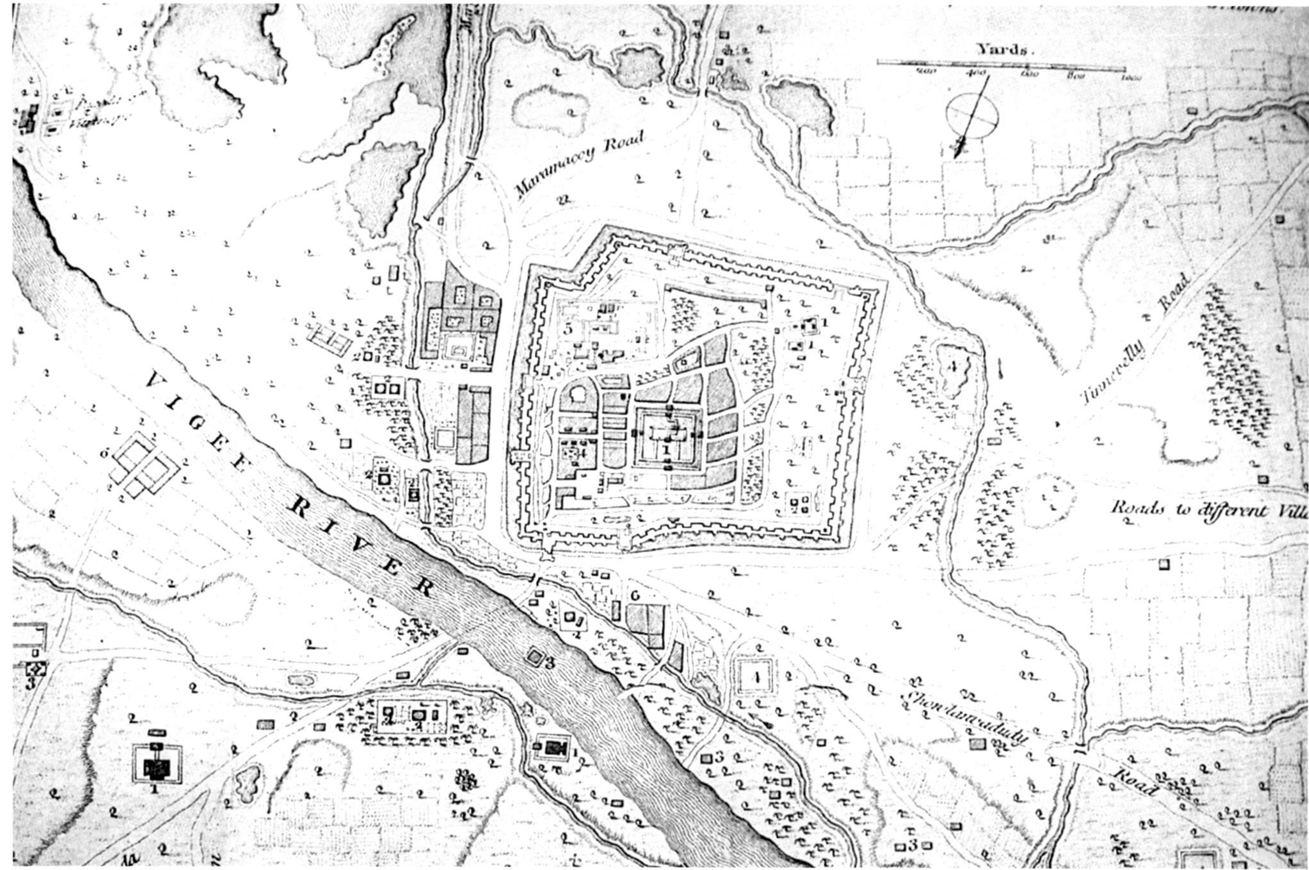

Map of Madurai during 1757 AD

Madurai as the capital of the Pandya clan finds mention in the *Sangam* work *Maduraikkanchi*. Madurai finds mention in the works of Roman historians Pliny the younger and Ptolemy and those of the Greek geographer Strabo. It is also mentioned in the Periplus of the Erythraean Sea. The city is also described extensively in the epic *Silapathikaram* dated to belong to the first few centuries of the christian era.

The Madurai Meenakshi temple or more correctly *"The Aalavay Annal Meenakshsi Chokkalinga Peruman's* temple" has four streets around it forming a square and resembles an attractive lotus. Later these streets obtained their association with the festivals pertaining to four tamil months and came to be called *Aadi Veedhi (Aadi Street), Chitthirai Veedhi, Aavani Veedhi* and *MaasiVeedhi.* During the *Maasi* festival the streets around which Meenakshi *Ther* (chariot) went around was given the name *MaasiVeedhi.* The *Aavani Moolam* festival gave the name *Aavani Moola Veedhi* to another and the same naming style applied to the other streets as well. Thus these four streets had beautifully built skyscrapers even during that period and hence the name *"Naan Maadak Koodal"* was given to this city.

Even to this day Madurai can boast of the Lower Entry-Point *(Keezh Vaasal)* and other entry-points *(Vaasal)* from the South, North and another from

Southern Gopuram, front view, Madurai 1895 AD

Aerial View of Gopuram during late 70"s

the Higher level - all of these being positional or directional in nature. These four entrances along with the Fort with its huge walls and the moat were in existence well into the British period. Whatever was seen outside the Fort was known as *Veli-Veedhi* (that which was outside). The present day parlance continues to use the names Lower *Veli-Veedhi*, Higher *Veli-Veedhi*, and *Veli-Veedhi's* from the North and South. These then perhaps circumscribed the Moat and the Fort.

Many street names in Madurai have their indelible connection with history and the *puranas*. The names are in vogue even today such as *Yaanaikkal* (Elephant-Stone) and *Simmakkal,* (Lion-Stone) *Velliambala-Theru* (a street after the temple made of silver), *Pittuth Thoppu Theru, Ezhukadal-Theru* (named after the rising sea), *Annakkuzhi Mandapam* (Food-Spot Mandapam), *Valaiveesi Theppakkulam* (Net-Cast Float-Festival Pond) - all these reminding us of the glorious sporting deeds of Lord *Thiru Aalavaai Peruman* and the functions associated with them. We will see some of these deeds sculpted in stone later on in this work.

From ancient to modern times Madurai has remained a prosperous religious and cultural centre where *Saivism* and Tamil literature had their roots and periodic revivals. This temple among all the temples of Tamil Nadu continues to be the most living temple forming the heart and soul of the entire city.

Artistic View of East Masi Street

Artistic View of East Masi Street 1792 AD

View of the Golden Lotus Tank 1895 AD

Legend

Every Hindu temple is unique and usually has a divine origin,that can be unravelled from the various legends surrounding it replete with mystic deeds of the presiding Lord.

Madurai too has its share of interesting legends associated with it, the most famous by far, being the legend of its favourite daughter - Meenakshi.

This legend portrays and glorifies her display of valour, leadership, courage, grace, modesty, and bashfulness - an embodiment of perfection.

Effacing of Indra's Sin

The first of the *Puranas* refers to the origins of Madurai and the divine association of the Meenakshi Sundareshwara temple. Hinduism has strong belief in reincarnation and the principle of *karma* - that the acts of one life have ramifications not only in the afterlife but also in the next birth. As a consequence great emphasis is laid on leading a pure sin-free life and in the

event where a sin is committed, they go through severe austerities for purification and cleansing. This is where the divine powers of Madurai come to rescue as illustrated in an interesting tale where, not only humans, but even Gods and Demi gods can seek cleansing in its sacred environs.

The first anecdote deals with an episode where Indra's sin is effaced. The legend goes thus: Indra, the Chief of Devas, had to kill a demon who was terrorising the three worlds for which he waged a war against the *Asuras*. Unfortunately the demon was a high born Brahmin, whose slaying brought upon Indra a grave sin. Indra tried various means to rid himself of the sin, but to no avail. Once, in the realm of humans, passing through a forest of *Kadamba* trees, Indra felt the burden being miraculously lifted. Relieved of his sin, he looked for the source and found a *Shiva Linga* of incomparable beauty and exceptional prowess, in the shades of the *Kadamba* tree. Next to the tree was a Golden Lily pond, wherein Indra proceeded to cleanse himself by bathing in its waters and offering the golden lily to the *Shiva Linga*.

Birth of Meenakshi

Once, Madurai was ruled by a King by name Malayadhvaja Pandian. His wife was Kaanchanamaalai and unfortunately they were not blessed with a child for quite a long period. They conducted a Yaga (an act of propitiation to the Gods), called *Puthra Kameshti Yagam*. A beautiful three year old female child was granted to them which appeared from the fire of the *Yaga*, spontaneously. This child had three breasts in its body and this caused distress to the royal couple, Malayadhvajan and Kaanchanamaalai. Also,they had asked God Almighty for a male child who could carry on the affairs of the Kingdom and they beseeched help from the God again. There was a voice from heaven that spoke thus, "Do not think that this is an ordinary female child. Nurture it the way you would treat a male child and make her the Queen; and when she sees her suitor one breast of hers will automatically disappear." They named the child Thadathagai and took abundant care in bringing her up. At the appropriate time, she was crowned the Queen of Madurai. From that day onwards she held the sceptre of royal power and ruled over Madurai.

Sculpture of Lord Meenakshi at the Pudumandapam

Meenakshi's encounter with Shiva

Thadathagai who ruled Madurai wanted to conquer the whole world and ventured boldly with her army in all directions. After conquering all of Heaven and Earth, finally she reached Mount Kailash in order to involve Lord Shiva in a battle. Lord Shiva was informed of this matter by Nandi and he readied himself to confront Thadathagai. As she faced Lord Shiva one to one, Thadathagai became shy and the middle of her three breasts disappeared. Her minister Sumathi reminded her of the voice from heaven that had predicted this to happen. This symbolises the principle that one can approach God only when the central ills of life namely Ego, Illusion and Pride disappear completely.

Lord Shiva appeared in Madurai as Somasundarar and married Thadathagai, who was none other than Meenakshiammai. The master of ceremonies, the *purohit*, was Brahmadeva, who performed the marriage rituals and the *yaga*. Meenakshi's brother Lord Vishnu poured the ceremonial water to solemnize the marriage and this was celebrated with the blessings of all assembled and to the happiness of all the three worlds.

Sculpture of Lord Shiva at the Pudumandapam

Celestial Wedding

Lord Shiva and Thadaathagai returned to Madurai where the King had organised the coronation of his daughter to be followed by her marriage to Lord Shiva the next day. It was to be arranged in the grandest possible fashion with the entire population on attendance. Scholars, poets, artists, artisans, kings and queens and people from all walks of life were all invited to the great event without discrimination.

Devas, Gandharvas, Vidyadharas, Rishis and Siddhas were also in the invitees' list. All roads led to Madurai and a huge congregation assembled there as if Madurai suddenly became the centre of the Universe.

Vishnu, the brother of Meenakshi was proceeding to Madurai from *Vaikuntam*, his abode in heaven, for *Kannika-dhanam* (bestowing the bride to the groom) when his passage was delayed by a trick played by Lord Indra. Vishnu saw through the deception and manifested himself in both places at the same time. He managed to preside over the marriage ceremony and perform *kannika-dhanam* ritual in the form of Thirupparadundram *Pavalakkanivaip-perumal*. This is being celebrated even to this day as Chithirai Thiruvizha (Chithirai Festival). During the rule of Thirumalai Nayakar, this was linked to Kallazhagar and became part of Azhagar Festival.

Sporty Deeds of the Lord *(Thiruvilaiyadal Legends)*

The great temple at Madurai is considered as one of the holiest of Shiva temples. Lord Shiva, in the form of Sundareshwarar is believed to have performed 64 *lilas* (Sport) here. These *lilas* dwell upon the divine intervention of Lord Shiva himself who had come down to the call of his devotees and performed miraculous deeds. These anecdotes are full of wit and wisdom, illustrating the Lord's compassion to his devotees. These devotees included kings, queens and the common man whose devotion to Lord Shiva was all consuming. Occasionally it reached such a height as to make the devotee offer his life and soul entirely to the Lord. Shiva donned several forms for the sake of devotees appearing as a *Siddhar*, a poet, a fisherman, a wood cutter and even a labourer.

The stories are narrated in various *sthalapuranams* pertaining to the Madurai temple. They became so popular that they have been written in various languages in different periods including the most elaborate versions such as Paranjothi's *Thiruvilaiyadal Puranam*. Some of the earliest among these *Puranas* are Perumbatrappuliyur

Nambi's *Thiruvalavayudaiyar Thiruvilaiyadal Puranam* and *Halasya Mahatmyam* a Sanskrit work based on the earlier *Puranams*. Nambi's work may be assigned to about the 12th-13th Century while Paranjothi's was written in the 16th -17th Century.

Other works in which the *Thiruvilaiyadal Lilas* are narrated are Andari's *Sundara Pandiyam* based on a Sanskrit work of the same name; *Ashtamipradaksina Manmyam* (both in Sanskrit and Tamil) and *Maduraikkalambakam* of Kumaraguruparar.

A large number of the *lilas* such as those connected with Thirugnanasambandar, the Jains, Manikkavacakar, the Cheras and the Cholas, are legends surrounding actual historical events. But at present, it is difficult to separate the fact from fiction completely. Apart from these minor and perhaps major differences, there is a lot of similarity about the various *lilas*.

Thiru Aalavai

Sale Of Firewood

Founding A Sacred City

Birth Of Ukkirapandian

Salvation to a Stork

This legendary story is somewhat unique, wherein the grace of Shiva is showered even on a bird. In this case a Stork, which is in search of fish to feed on, chances to find a lake where a few hermits are performing their ablutions. It overhears their talk about the sanctity of Madurai and wishes to see the place. Upon visiting the sacred temple, it comes to the famous Golden Lotus pond, where a fish jumps near it. The nature of the stork is to feed on the fish, but that would vilify the sacred campus and so curtails its natural instincts. Whereupon Shiva reveals himself to it and appreciates this selfless quality of the bird. He blesses it with release from the cycle of birth and death and grants Godhood. The Stork further implores on him, to assist future avian visitors who might not be able to control their senses as well as itself. Shiva in all his grace grants that wish as well and causes that there would be no marine life in the golden lotus pond, henceforth.

Sugarcane to Stone Elephant

The sacred confines of the temple find mention again in another episode of the *Thiruvilayadal*. Shiva comes disguised as a mendicant performing a lot of miracles in the temple. Word of his deeds reaches the King, who summons him for an audience. Shiva promptly ignores the summon, saying that his place is only amongst the devotees. Enraged the King himself comes to the temple and challenges him to show him his prowess. He takes a sugarcane and asks the Mendicant to feed one of the stone elephants that stand around the Sanctum. The Lord promptly offers it to the stone elephant, which, to the surprise and utter amazement of all present, comes alive, trumpets loudly, extends its trunk to take the sugarcane and proceeds to eat it. Finally it turns back to stone, by which time the Pandya King realises the true identity of the Mendicant and falls at his feet. Having accomplished his task the Lord disappears after showering his blessings on the king.

Sculpture of Lord Shiva as mendicant giving sugarcane to the stone elephant at the Pudumandapam

Saivite Savants *(Naalvar)*

The *Thevaram* trinity, namely Thiru Gnanasambandar, Tirunavukarasar and Sundarar during the seventh and eighth centuries paved the way for the spread of Saivism. Their discovery of its deep rooted traditions threw light on the entire culture itself. In their pilgrimages in Tamil Nadu, they had visited all Saivite shrines with ancient traditions and sung hymns in praise of the presiding deity.

Koon Pandian alias Nedumaran the Pandiyan ruler was converted to Jainism. With royal patronage, Jainism spread its net and for its effective propagation, Jain monks had camped in the eight hillocks around Madurai. To prevent Saivism's total eclipse Queen Mangayarkkarasiar and Minister Kulachirayar invited Saint Gnanasambandar to visit them at Madurai. The Saint visited Madurai, prayed to the deity and performed a lot of miracles. The king understood that all these could happen only with divine blessings of Lord Shiva. Upon seeing all these miraculous deeds and realising the powers of Saivism, King reconverted to the Saiva fold.

Thiruneetru Padhigam of Thiru Gnana Sambanthar

The ten hymns about the sanctity and powers of the sacred ash (*Thiruneeru*) is a unique contribution to Tamil Devotional Literature. Although it is easily understood, simple and lucid, there is a central theme covering the elements of Saiva theology, in their proper and logical order. One can easily miss it if not properly studied.

The hymn is in praise of the sacred ash. King Nedumaran was suffering from serious stomach ache and all the medics could not cure it. Thiru Gnanasambandar applied the sacred ash which miraculously cured the painful disease he was suffering from. This powerful miracle inspired the king to change over from Jainism to Saivism. From beginning to end this *padhigam* deals with life from a larger perspective. In the language of Saivites the term sacred ash (*Thiruneeru*) represents a multi dimensional life- symbol of the individual spirit, all the time seeking to discover its relationship amidst the laws and forces of earthly life, with universal spirit. Here the word sacred ash (*thiruneeru*) repeatedly occurs in a formula as it were, carrying a connotation of an inner force struggling to reach and mingle with the universal spirit. The hymn therefore is a panacea for not only external well being but also internal well being of the soul, not only for King Nedumaran but also any one who recites it.

Tirunavukarasar, a contemporary of Gnanasambandhar also visited the temple. His *thevaram* songs with the divine influence of Lord Shiva offer a glimpse of the temple and throws light on the magnificence of the temple and its grandeur. It infused life into the kingdom and brought prosperity to the people of Madurai.

Sundarar, another contemporary of Thiru Gnanasambandhar has many credits as a true devotee of Lord Shiva. In one instance Lord Shiva appears before him after he calls the Lord a mad man. When Sundarar realises it the Lord asks him to compose a hymn with *pitha* (madman) as the starting word.

Manikkavasakar, an eighth century poet and the last of the four Saivite Savants, was born in Thiruvadavur and became a minister in the Court of Varaguna Varman II (860-880 AD). He was given a lot of money and sent on a mission to purchase horses and on the way God himself came as an ascetic, became his Guru and blessed him with *Shivagnanam*. Filled with gratitude and devotion to Shiva, he built a beautiful temple in Thiruperundurai with the money he brought for the horses. When the king learnt of the misdeed, he wanted to punish Manikkavasakar. The Lord heeding to the prayers of his devotee, turned the horses into foxes to pacify the king, but when they turned back to foxes, the enraged King punished the Saint by roasting him in the Vaigai sand. The Lord once again intervened and caused floods in Vaigai to save the devotee. The King realised his mistake and became a disciple of the Saint Manickavasagar. For sheer love of the Supreme Lord there are no other poems to equal the *Thiruvasagam* and *Thirukkovaiyar* of Saint Manickavasagar full of poignant outpouring of *jeevatma* in the yearning for the *Paramatma*.

Goddess Meenakshi
The Presiding Deity

Angayarkanni, the beautiful name of Goddess Meenakshi in Tamil, comes from *am+kayal+kanni* meaning one with beautiful fish-like eyes. The word Meenakshi also denotes the same; *meen* referring to fish and *akshi* referring to the eyes. Just as the fish has no eyelids and is therefore always awake, it may be said poetically that the divine mother Meenakshi is eternally awake to protect all creation. The pleasing eyes, the warm smile, the elegant posture, shapely arms and ornamental decoration are unique to the Goddess. Nowhere can one see such a divine deity with so much of grace in Tamil Nadu. This deity lends a special flavour to the city of Madurai along with the Tamil culture that is omnipresent here. The different decorations of the Goddess during various festive occasions are a pleasure never to be missed.

The name and fame that Madurai city obtained over the centuries and the well-being of its citizens are, according to belief, entirely due to the presence of the temple in the centre of the city and the presiding Goddess Meenakshi. It went to the extent of being accorded the status of one of the Wonders of the World.

The image of the Goddess is in a standing posture with the right arm carrying a flower and the left arm suspended along the body. A green parrot is seated on the right shoulder and the face beams with resplendent beauty. The ornamental *Kireetam* (crown) is in conformity with the Nayakar hairstyle, with the left side *kondai* (hairdo) traditionally known as *Mambazhakkondai* (Mango shaped chignon). The Goddess is seen with the right foot slightly forward of the left foot as if about to walk towards the devotees.

The figure of Goddess Meenakshi is a perfect blend of beauty, grace, benevolence and poise: the facial expression revealing shyness as if she is awaiting her Lord's arrival. The parrot on her right hand and the gracefully suspended left arm have been the subject of adulation by inspired poets. The shining attire with multi coloured garlands enhances the brilliance of her bejewelled ornaments. The high-rise crown set with precious stones, the look of compassion in the face, leisurely standing posture all add to the divinity of the image of Goddess making the devotees experience sanctity and peace in her presence.

The Sanctum Sanctorum Meenakshi Shrine

The Meenakshi shrine and its *Prakarams* are smaller than those of the Sundareshwarar shrine. Nevertheless it excels in inspiring devotion and awe among its devotees. The *garbhagriha* of the sanctum is almost a square measuring about 25 feet each side with the *ardha mandapam* on its front. It measures about 25 feet by 45 feet. This measurement may have been planned but then for a sanctum sanctorum to be planned by mere mortals is no mean accomplishment. It takes divine intervention to house the goddess in such a place.

The masonry work speaks volumes about the artisans involved. Blessed are those souls whose hands built the shrine from stone. The sculptors had invoked the divine magic of sculpting to create a splendor such as this. Hands that sculpted the architectural beauty must have been blessed by the Lord himself - such finesse, such precision and such a degree of symmetry!

The *garbhagriha* entrance has a Gajalakshmi panel on its beam under a *thoranam*. This feature is unique since a welcome by the elephants is auspicious.

The *ardha mandapam* has a plain interior and there are no pillars in it. This gives an impression of space to the interior of the *Mandapam*. As is customary to all Hindu temples in Tamil Nadu, two four-armed *dvarapalakas* are at the entrance to the *ardha mandapam*. This enables the devotees to view the deity from far off without any hindrance. Four modern pillars support a small entrance mandapam on the east wall of the *ardha mandapam*.

The *garbhagriha* walls have three projecting bays with niches. These have short pilasters at the corners and semi-pilasters at the niche openings. In the niche of the central bay on the south is the image of *Ichashakthi*, that on the west has *Kriyashakthi* while that on the north has *Gnanashakthi*. It is believed that the presence of these shakthis gives strength to the devotee to conquer time, or *kaala*.

The *maha mandapam* has six rows of pillars forming a central nave and three aisles on either side. The pillars of the aisles are of the ordinary cubical type. But they have a set pattern that makes it look pleasing to the viewer.

The image of Meenakshi in the Sanctum is one of the most graceful yet powerful icons ever sculpted. No ordinary hands could have sculpted it. It must have been blessed with all the divine grace of the Goddess. The singular grace of the divine bride beautifully contrasts her earlier boyish charm. It's a ravishing treat for the devotee to catch a glimpse of the blushing new bride resplendent in her wedding finery. The attire and the ornaments go well with the slight shy smile on the deity's face.

Facing the *gopuram* is the *arukal pitham* of the shrine. At the south-east corner of this corridor is the stucco figures of Thirumalai Nayakar and his queens facing the *kolu* mandapam in the south-west corner at the other end of the southern *prakaram*. The Navarathri festival is celebrated in this mandapam. To the north of the kolu mandapam is the *Kadaka Gopuram*. On the other side of the *Kadaka gopuram* in the north-west corner of the *prakaram* is the *Kudal Kumarar* (Subramanya) shrine.

On the whole it can be said that the sanctum sanctorum is in itself a divine abode for the deity. If she is shyly standing in wait for the Lord then it is our privilege that we bow and pray to her seeking her blessing for the entire world to prosper. For, if she can do wonders to the city of Madurai with her presence there, she would be willing to fulfill all our prayers too.

The right angle view of the Amman shrine with its artistic sculptures and pillars

Dancing damsels adorn the sides of the platform

The carvings atop the sanctum are excellent work of sculptural excellence

The Lord's resting chamber with its beautifully carved metal door.

The architectural beauty can be seen in the dancing figurines at the base. It possesses such symmetry and liveliness that upon entering one is drawn towards it. The *Arukal Pitham* has four pillars in the front and one each on the two sides. The two central pillars on the front have large *yali* figures and there are stone chains going inside through the rings hanging from upper part of the pillar. It looks as if the stone chain has been fastened to the rings.

The additional feature noticeable on the wall surface are structures called *kumbapancarams* resembling waterpots with slender shafts in the *palliyarai* (bed chamber) and the shrines of Vighneswara and Subrahmanyar which are in the sanctum are in the same style as the rest of the structure.

Kumara Gurupara Swamigal

Kumara Guruparar, a juvenile prodigy was a contemporary of Thirumalai Nayakar (1625-1659) in the 17th century. He was speechless till the age of six, and by the grace of Lord Murugan of Thiruchendur his faculty of speech was restored. Even at such a tender age, he spontaneously composed *Kandar Kali Venba* in praise of Lord Murugan of Thiruchendur. He visited Madurai probably at the invitation of Tirumalai Nayakar, and composed five poetical works in praise of Goddess Meenakshi, notable among them being *Meenakshi Ammai Pillaithamizh, Meenakshi Ammai Irattai Manimalai*, and *Meenakshi Kalambakam*.

A miracle is believed to have occurred during the *Arangetram* (inaugural performance) of *Meenakshi Ammai pillai thamizh* in the presence of Thirumalai Nayakar. Goddess Meenakshi herself in the form of the daughter of temple priest appeared and took a seat on the lap of Nayakar. When the particular verse starting *"thodukkum kadavut pazham padal"* was rendered by Kumara Guru Swamigal, Goddess Meenahshi took off the necklace of Thirumalai Nayakar, offered it to *Swamigal* and vanished. Devotees of Meenakshi Amman even today render these songs with a lot of involvement during special occasions of worship

Depiction of Meenakshi Pillai Tamil

The Gold Sikharam is one of the most beautiful and impressive works in the entire Temple. The Golden pinnacle of Amman sanctum was installed by Siramalai Sevanthi Murthy Chetti in the year 1559 AD

The golden vimanam has the Goddess figurine carved on it in such intricate fashion that the details in the metal can be seen from down below. This structure offers a breathtaking view of the sculptor's artwork.

Lord Sundareshwarar
(*Chokkanathar*) –*The divine consort*

Chokkanatha Peruman manifested himself variously as a Siddha, a poet, a king, a slave, a soldier and even an animal and enacted several *Thiruvilayadals* (divine sports) in Madurai. The Lord is known for such games that He has enacted either for the sake of pampering the Goddess or for pacifying her anger. Since the deity has appeared on its own (*Suyambhu*) it is worshiped also by the Devas. The *Lingam* is surrounded by twenty seven lamps at the back that denote the stars in the Hindu monthly calender. The snake shaped crown and the sight of the pompous deity gives goose pimples to the viewer.

The deity is known as Sundareshwarar, Meenakshi Sundarar, Somasundarar, Kalyana Sundarar, Shanbaga Sundarar, Attavai Shevagan, Chockalingam, Adiyarku Nallan, Adhiraveesi, Vilayaduvan, Abhideka Chockar, Azhagiya Chockar, Kadambavana Chockar, Puzhugu Neidhu Chockar, Kadambavaneswarar, Karpoora Chockar, Madureswarar, Irayanar, Peralavayar and many other names.

The Sanctum Sanctorum - Lord Shiva Shrine

The sanctum of the Sundareshwarar shrine, surrounded by the sculptures depicting the entire *Thiruvilayadal* (Divine sport) takes us through the corridors of history. The colorful depiction of the story brings one's imagination to life. The details in the sculptures have not left out the expressions of the characters in the story. Nowhere else is seen *Dwarapalakas* beckoning us when we enter the sanctum. The huge 12 feet figures tower over the entrance that gives the feeling of the strong presence of the Lord inside

The sanctum is a square structure, the exterior walls measuring 33 ft, on all four sides. On the south, west and north sides of the walls of the *garbhagriha* are three bays or shrines which project six feet from the wall surface. The shrine in the

The panoramic view of the shrine offers a majestic sight of the temple

south is dedicated to Daksinamurthi, that on the west has Lingodbhavar while the one on the north has Durgai. The Sanctum is a small cubicle while the wall of the *garbhagriha* is a thick one. The *Swayambhu lingam* occupies the centre of the *garbhagriha* and the figure of *Manonmani*, facing south, occupies the north-east corner of the sanctum. A narrow passage about four feet long leads from the sanctum to the *antharalam* which is a little over 8 feet wide. Close to the line where the *Ardha Mandapam* joins the sanctum is a beautiful stone-pierced window in a niche in the north and south walls. The window opening has its own short semi-pilasters and a decoration over its beam. The *Ardha Mandapam* floor rises to a level just below the *kumudam* of the *adhisthanam* of the *garbhagriha*. So the base of the *garbhagriha* below the Kumudam is covered by the floor of the *Ardha Mandapam* and cannot be seen. The *adhisthanam* of the *ardha mandapam*

The gigantic 12 feet Dwarapalakas seen at the entrance of the Sanctum

has the same mouldings as the *garbhagriham* and the same kind of wall pilasters, corbels and cornice. But there are no niche openings though short niche pilaster with a cornice and a pavilion with roof and central decorate the wall surface. The cornices of these wall niches have the same kind of simulated timber work as on the under-surface of the main cornice surrounding the wall.

Lord Sundareshwara is personified in the sanctum sanctorum as the *Shiva Lingam* which is considered to be the very one worshiped by Devendra. He is known as" *Thiru aalavayudaiya Nayanar* or *Tambiran* in the temple epigraphs and records. The '*Kalladam*" a Tamil literary work of 9th century AD refers to the Madurai Temple and *Lilas* performed by Lord Sundareshwara. It mentions the *Indra Vimanam* with the '*ashtagajas*' and says God of *Aalavai* who is called the *Mula Kaaranan*' resided there with Goddess Uma (Meenakshi).

A niche is on either side of these three central shrines. Each niche is filled by a large stone-elephant measuring about ten feet high. These elephants are finely sculptured, look realistic and are very impressive. There are slight variations in the ornaments carved on them and in the material held in their trunks. These variations give them a certain individuality. According to legend the *vimanam* in which Somasundareswarar is enshrined was known as *Indravimanam* as it was made to the order of Indra by Visvakarman. The *vimanam* is supported by the guardian elephants of the eight directions. Six of them are seen on the exterior walls and the remaining two are close to the east wall of the *garbhagriha* within the *ardha mandapam*.

The *vimanam* repeats in all its three storeys, in the projections and recesses on the *garbhagriham* walls. Though it has been renewed a number of times and many stucco figures have been either altered or added, the essential characteristics of an earlier structure have been retained.

The stucco figures, though numerous, do not detract from the main lines of the edifice. The gold-plated *vimanam* is one of the most beautiful and impressive parts in the whole temple. In front of the *ardhamandapam* is a *mukhamandapam* constructed by Kulasekara Pandiyan in 12th century. The door way leading from this *mukhamandapam* to the *ardhamandapam* has a Gajalakshimi panel on the lintel. As mentioned earlier the presence of gajalakshmi is considered auspicious. On either side of this door way in the *mukhamandapam* are two *dwarapalakas*. Next to the *dwarapalaka* is Vallabha Ganapathi on the south and next to the *dwarapalakas* on the opposite side is an image of Subrahmanyar on the peacock. Two doorways on the northern and southern side of the *mukhamandapam* lead to the first *prakaram*. Four pillars form a square in the centre of the *mukhamandapam*. The *mukhamandapam* leads to the large *mahamandapam*.

The *mahamandapam* measures about 55 feet in width and 85 feet in length. This was also constructed by Kulasekara Pandiyan and renovated during Nayak period. There are four projecting bays on each of the exterior sides of the four walls of the *mahamandapam*. The *adhistanam* of the *mahamandapam* differs slightly from that of the *garbhagriha*. The walls of the *mahamandapam* are decorated with many stucco panels illustrating the 64 *Thiruvilaiyadal* legends.

Although they have been constructed many centuries ago, it is a place that one must visit at least once in lifetime. The extravagant coloring and pomp surrounding the temple structures makes one stare in awe. There may have been temples built before and after, but this one temple is a must to be seen and relished as an architectural marvel.

The sculptures around the Sanctum speak of the excellence and finesse with
which the sculptors have recreated the Divine Sport.

This pinnacle is designed with 8 elephants, 32 lions and 64 Sivaganas (divine attendants) that is unique to this temple sanctum. This feature is not available in any of the other ancient temples of Dravidian culture

Sundareshwarar Shrine - its architectural beauty

Lord Sundareshwarar is embodied in a *Lingam* form in the sanctum sanctorum in the Madurai temple. The construction of the *vimanam* (tower over the sanctum sanctorum) conforms to the description in the *Sthala Puranam* (temple history). Along the peripheral walls of the sanctum one can see majestic sculptures of elephants. This is known as *Indira Vimanam* (the tower of Indira the lord of the Devas). One can see the rare structure of the eight elephants known as *Ashta Diggajangal*, supporting the *vimanam* along the eight directions. This Indira *Vimanam* finds mention in the book *Aalavay Mahanmiyam* written by Paranjothi Munivar which describes 64 divine sports (*thiruvilayadal*) of Sundareshwarar. In Perumpatrappuliyur Nambi's *Thiruvilayadal Purana* it is mentioned that the area that is now Madurai was a forest of Kadamba trees and during Indira's visit he saw an image of Chokkanathar exposed to the elements. He was moved by the sight and decided to provide an appropriate shrine to lord Chokkanathar. He ordered Maya, the divine engineer to bring an exquisite *vimana* on the back of eight elephants and offered it to Sundareshwarar – hence the name Indira vimanam. It is believed that through this act of devotion Indira was delivered of the sin of killing the demon Vrittrasura.

The golden pinnacle or Indira Vimanam or Ashtagaja vimanam said to have been installed by none other than Indira himself. This pinnacle was given a gold plating by Viswanatha Nayakar (1559 - 63 AD)

The blazing golden vimanam is gleaming with brightness shining atop the shrine.

Velli Amballam

This is one of the five royal courts (*Sabai or Sabha*) where Lord Shiva is worshipped as Nataraja, performing his Cosmic Dance. The Tamil word 'Velli' means Silver and '*Ambalam*' means Stage or altar. This Shiva shrine also consists of an unusual sculpture of Nataraja. This massive Nataraja sculpture is enclosed in a huge silver altar and hence called '*Velli Ambalam*' (The Silver abode). The famous Hindu marquee and a dancing form of Shiva that normally has his left foot raised, has his right foot raised in this temple. According to the *Tiruvilayaadal Puranam*, this is on the request of Rajasekara Pandya, who was a sincere devotee of Lord Shiva. Being an expert of dancing, the King felt that the Lord was subjecting himself to enormous stress by dancing on the same leg and out of love for him, pleaded with him to change his stance. Pleased with his devotion Shiva changed his pose and is seen here dancing on his right foot – called *Maarukaal Thandavam*.

The colorful stucco figures depict the Divine Sport all around the sanctum

Safeguarding the idols during the invasion

After Maravarman Kulasekara Pandian's death (1268 -1310) there was a civil war between his two sons Jatavarman Sundara Pandian and Jatavarma Veera Pandian. Moreover the plundering raids of Malik Kafur and Khusru led to the rapid disintegration of the Pandya Empire. This paved the way for the establishment of a Muslim sultanate at Madurai. Sundara Pandian sought the help of Malik Kafur in his struggle with his brother.

The Tamil Chronicles indicate how the temple at Madurai suffered vandalism under the Muslim rule. The Madurai *Sthanikar Varalaru* gives a detailed account of the tribulations of the time. The *Sthanikars* (trustees) of the temple made a *Kilikkundu* for the Swami in the *garbhagriha*. Raised earth mounds blocked the *garbhagriha* entrance and built a stone wall to protect the original *lingam* from the invaders. Further a replica of the original *lingam* was set up in the *Ardha mandapam*. They also performed

ashtabandhanam for the goddess (*moola peru Nachiyar*) and set up the Goddess on the upper story of the *Vimanam*. They further carried out *Pupadanam* (burying in the ground) for the idols near the *Muchukundeswars* shrine.

The replica lingam that was damaged by Malik Kafur. (this lingam saved the original lingam from the invaders)

Dismembering of Chittan

There was a teacher of martial arts in Madurai by name Baanan who was running a school for training students in sword fight. Though he was of advanced age he was training quite and a few students one of whom was Chittan. Chittan started a new school for sword fight in competition to Banan taking away much of the business. Not stopping with that, Chittan coveted Baanan's wife and the good lady being a devotee of Somasundara Peruman appealed to the Lord to teach Chittan a lesson. Somasundarar in deference to the prayer of Baanan's wife took the form of Baanan himself and challenged Chittan for a sword fight. Chittan readily accepted thinking it would be a cakewalk. In the fight Lord in the form of Banan fought so well to everybody's amazement and cut off Chittan's limbs one by one before finally disappearing. Baanan returning from his routine temple visit, learnt of this *leela* (sport) of the Lord from his students. Everyone was overcome with awe and amazement at this *leela* (divine sport) of the Lord and praised his compassion towards his devotees. During the Avani Moolam passion festival Somasundarar is decked up in the attire of a sword fighter who fought for Baanan on the sixth day of the festival.

The 51 Lingam Images known as Akshara Lingam located on the north of Sanctum of lord Sundareshwarar

The 63 Nayanmars in Lord Sundareshwarar Shrine

Ellam valla siddhar
(The all powerful saint)

The image of *Ellam Valla Siddhar* is located in the northwest corner on the periphery of the sanctum of Lord Sundareshwarar. *Siddhi* denotes liberation from the bondage of Karma and attainment of several yogic powers on the path to self realization. Lord Shiva himself appeared as a *Siddha* and blessed his devotees and these places acquired the name *Siddheswaram's*.

In *Thiruvilaydal Puranam* Lord Sundareshwarar performed Miracles and became known as *Ellam Valla Siddhar*.

The image of *Ellam Valla Siddhar* is seen displaying *Chinmudra* with right hand while clasping the yoga *danda* with the left. His matted hair is gathered together in a chignon on top of the head. He is seen seated in a pose of *Veerasana* facing eastern direction. The *Panchaloha* (made of five metals and alloys) idol of the *siddhar* which is placed in the *mahamandapam* is seen with a magic wand in the right hand. This is often taken to denote a sugarcane piece by some and in the Temple festival in the month of *'thai'* a festival is organized to mark the feeding of the stone elephant with sugarcane as narrated in *Thiruvilayadal Puranam*

Inscription on Rhythm and Music

The two stone inscriptions relating to thirty five rhythms, *Saptha Suladhi* rhythm and *Simhanandana* rhythm at Madurai temple record a continuity of music and dance traditions which seem to be taking a deeper root with the times. The *angas* (elements) of the *Saptha suladhi* rhythm and *Simhanandana* rhythm are detailed in musical notations in the floral sculptural inscriptions found in two pillars facing each other in the six pillars mandapam behind the Chandeswarar shrine in the second *prakara* of Lord's sanctum. The inscriptions go a long way to explain the importance given to music during this period. Acoustics were accorded equal importance along with artful exhibition of sculptures.

Vibuthi Pillayar

A uniqueness to this temple is the presence of the ash smeared elephant god. To the south of the pond (*Potramarai Kulam*) and more towards the west one can see the *Vibuthi Pillayar,* quite popular among devotees. Those who come to this temple make it a routine to worship this Pillayar first, before proceeding to worship Meenakshi-Sundareshwarar. Standing before this elephant deity and worshipping him is of recent origin. The traditional practice would involve worshipping Meenakshi before Sundareshwarar. It is worth mentioning here, that in order to apply sacred ash (*vibuthi*) before applying vermilion (*kumkumam*) on their foreheads, the *vibuthi* from this Pillayar is considered auspicious.

The Panchaloha idol of Lord Chandikeswarar in a graceful pose.

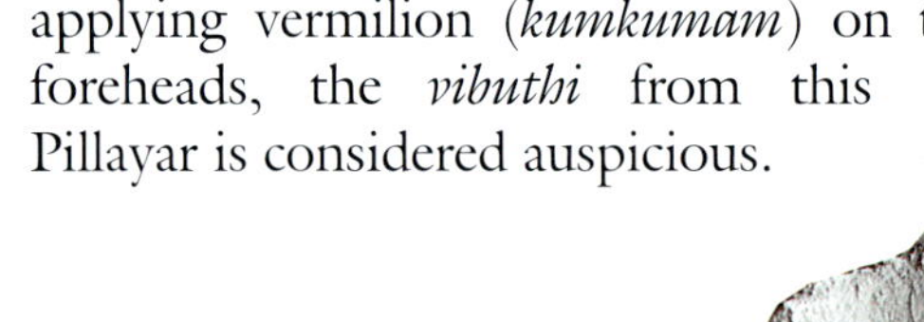

Age is no bar for worship. A little boy offering Vibuthi to the Lord Vibuthi Vinayagar.

Mukkuruni Pillayar

The *shrine* of Mukkuruni Pillayar on the Southern side of inner *gopuram* is a magnificent one rising to eight feet in height. *Pillayar* is seen with his four benevolent hands. About the year 1645 A.D, Thirumalai Nayakar planned and dug a huge float--festival-pond in the eastern side of Madurai. It is generally believed that this *Pillayar* came up during the digging process. There was probably a temple for this *Pillayar* in the area where Vandiyur Mariamman pond is presently positioned. It is quite possible that this temple was brought down during the invasions of Malik Kafur. Later when Thirumalai Nayakar dug up the pond, this statue may have been found, fortunately for humanity. But the manner and type of this statue does not seem to resemble those of the Pandya period, but is after those of the Naicker's reign. The holy installation of this *Pillayar* here was done by Kandhap Podi Pethhu Chettiar. Every year in the month of *Avani* (Tamil month) a special rice cake made out of the choicest rice (*mukkuruni*) is being offered to this God and hence the name Mukkuruni Pillayar.

The seven foot high idol of Mukkurini Vinayakar, carved in a single rock was installed by King Thirumalai Nayakar in the year 1645.

The panchaloka metal idol of Mukkuruni Vinayakar; the god of all auspicious beginnings.

Inscriptions

Temples were seen primarily as places of worship. But they also played a very important role for future generations, to get a glimpse into the history of Tamil Nadu. Temples served as Documentation Centers as well. The inscriptions and carvings are probably the first documentation techniques adopted by mankind which is true in case of Madurai Temple also. It often praises the hard work that has gone into making the temple by the kings and common man alike.

Saint Thirugnana Sambandar (8th century AD) has sung in praise of the Madurai Meenakshi temple in his Madurai *Thiruppadikam*. He refers to an extensive temple complex with a massive compound wall named *Kapaali* as the abode of *Aalavayan*. In later periods, the temple was expanded and embellished with additions and modifications by the earlier and later Pandiya Kings, King of Vijayanagaram, Vanadhirayar, Nayakars of Madurai and the British. The earliest inscriptions we have belong to 12th century. No inscriptions of the earlier periods of the Chola and Pandya ruled are now available. They may have been lost during renovations and expansions of the sanctum.

So far sixty four inscriptions have been identified and copied by the Archeological Survey of India out of which 44 belong to the later Pandiya periods. 19 to the period of Vijayanagaram Kings and one to the British period. Among the later Pandiya Kings whose contribution finds mention in the stone inscriptions are Sadaiyavarman Kulasekara Pandiyan I (1194 AD), Maravarman Sundara Pandiyan I (1216 – 1244 AD), Maravarman Sundara Pandiyan II (1238 – 1255 AD), Maravarman Vikrama Pandiyan II (1250 – 1276 AD), Kulasekara Pandiyan I (1268 – 1318), Sadayavarman Veerapandiyan III (1315 – 1384) and Parakrama Pandiyan. It was during the reign of Maravarman Sundara Pandiyan II that the temple grew significantly judging from the number of inscriptions during his period.

Among the Vijayanagara rulers, Krishnadeva Rayar (1509 – 1529), Achutha Devarayar (1529-1542 AD), Sadasiva Rayar (1542-1570) are mentioned in the inscriptions. Inscriptions are also available bearing the names of Veerappa Nayakar (1572-1595), Kumara Krishnappa Nayakar, Muthu Veerappa Nayakar (1609 – 1623), Thirumalai Nayakar (1623 – 1659 AD) and Vijayaranga Chokkanatha Nayakar (1706 – 1732). There is also one inscription of Pachayappa Mudaliyar belonging to 1842 AD during the British rule.

Heliographic inscriptions that shows the development of literature in that period itself

Golden Lotus Pond

Legend has it that Indra offered a golden lotus from this pond to Lord Shiva to absolve himself of the sin of killing Vrithrasura. The pond has no marine life on account of the boon that Lord Shiva granted to a stork as per an anecdote in *Thiruvilayadal*. This pond is believed to have acted as the judge in deciding the aesthetic merit of any literary work during Sangam period. A plank carrying the literary work would float if acceptable and sink if not worthy. The corridors around the pond have mural paintings of colourful depiction of the divine sports of Lord Sundareshwarar.

Lord Nataraja in a iconographic representation
of Shiva's cosmic Dance.

Iconographic Sculptures

The wealth of iconographic images found in the Madurai temple are helpful in offering an in depth insight into the study of Hindu mythology. It is doubtful whether any other temple in South India has the same multitude of carvings, stuccos and paintings of gods and goddesses as the Madurai temple possesses. "The one *mahatmyam* that has contributed very largely to the multiplication of images of Shiva is the *Halasya Mahatmyam* pertaining to God Shiva at Madurai, the capital of the Pandyas. It is no wonder then that the Meenakshi-Sundareshwarar temple and its neighborhood should be intimately connected with the many Shiva forms of the *agamas* and of the Shiva *Lilas* in the *puranas*. Some particular edifices are well known for the iconographic sculptures on their pillars: for instance, the *Kambatthadi Mandapam* and the Thousand Pillar Mandapam. The *Pudu Mandapam* has iconographic and mythological sculptures as well as portraits of the Nayakars. Many of the *gopurams* contain stuccos relating to the Saiva pantheon and *puranas*.

Golden idols of the Lord and the Goddess that is unique to this temple. It is considered a blessing to get a glimpse of these celestial idols.

Kambatthadi Mandapam

With all the celebrities from the three worlds descending upon earth for the occasion of the celestial wedding, this *mandapam* offers the best sculptures of Hindu mythology. The Kambatthadi Mandapam is famous for depicting all the 25 forms of Lord Shiva. Being situated just in front of main sanctum and containing as it does the Nandhi Mandapam and the *dwajasthambams*, it has all its sculptures relating only to Shiva forms. Going round the pillars one can notice the pillar on the left, the well known Meenakshi-Sundareshwarar marriage group. The sculpturing, though done as late as 1870, is a magnificent piece of Hindu craftsmanship and is in some ways better than a similar sculpture in the Pudu Mandapam which, of course, must have been done during Thirumalai Nayakar days. This scene shows Shiva standing on the right with his right hand just holding Meenakshi's right hand while Vishnu giving away his sister, ceremoniously shown by the way of pouring water as part of the *kannikadanam*, out of a pot. Behind the wedding group is sculptured a beautiful decorative tree. This is perhaps the *Karpaga Vriksham* presented to Meenakshi by Indra during her *digvijayam*. The expression on the three principal parties to the happy event is most beautifully rendered and one must note especially the shy face of Meenakshi which has yet an expressive smile. This picture of the celestial wedding finds its place in almost all the wedding functions of Tamil Nadu these days.

The sculptures speak of the divine atmosphere that prevailed at that time. All the faces in the sculptures show warmth and glow. It is a conglomeration of all the divinity in the three worlds that is depicted in a grand manner in this mandapam.

View of Kambatthadi Mandapam that houses the 27 forms of Shiva Manifestation

This mandapam houses Lord Shiva in all his 27 form. Visitors always make it a point to visit this important place for its rich show of heritage and sculptures.

Manifestation of Shiva

1 Kalyanasundarar
2 Tripurantakar
3 Suhasanar
4 Kalasamharar
5 Pasupathar
6 Natarajar
7 Kamadhahanar
8 Chandrasekarar
9 Umamaheswarar
10 Lingodhbavar
11 Gajamuka Anugrahar &
     Ravana Anugrahar
12 Chakradhanar
13 Ekapadar
14 Rishbharudar
15 Arthanari
16 Hariharar
17 Jalandaraauther
18 Dakshinamurthy
19 Gajasamharar
20 Sandesa Anugrahar
21 Bikshandhar
22 Veerabhadrar
23 Kiratha Arjunar
24 Rishabandakar
25 Somaskandar

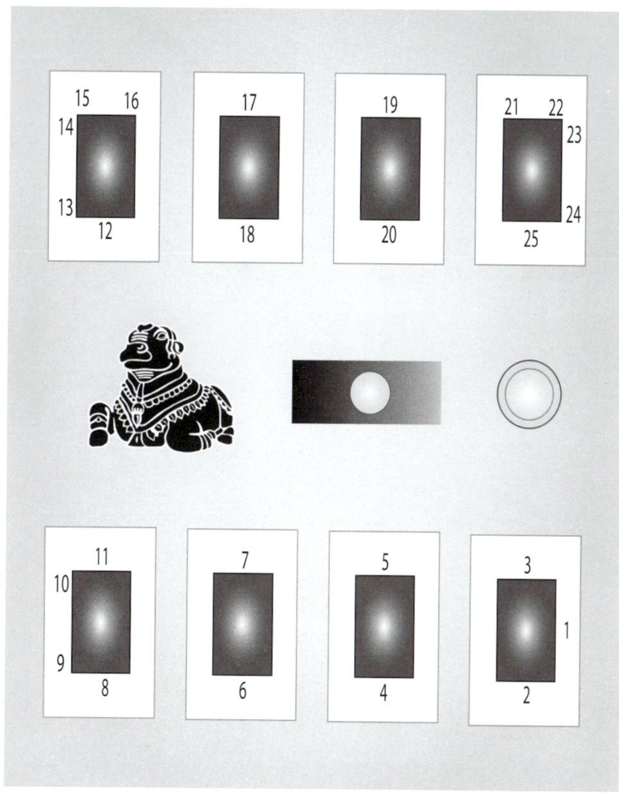

*The splashing water poured on Nandhi by a priest highlights
the belief that it cleanses one's soul. Nandhi Mandapam
surrounded by Shiva manifestations is built by
Krishna Veerappa Nayakar during 1564 AD*

Kalyanasundarar

This is probably the most extravagant sculpture of its kind that depicts the Hindu wedding ritual in a very descriptive manner. Nowhere can such a sculpture be found that involves the celestial ritual. Shiva is an eternal bridegroom and *Sakthi* is the eternal bride. In every Shiva temple Shiva's wedding is celebrated annually to show that Shiva weds Uma to bless the universe. The wedding of Shiva and Uma was needed for the birth of Kumara to destroy the demons. Shiva and Sakthi are depicted as immortal lovers. Their wedding is the union of Truth (Shiva) and wisdom (Sakthi) as a result of which Ananda (Skanda) is born. Lord Shiva is known as Kalyana Sundara Murthy with the wedding of Uma. This form is the model for the human race to follow and to lead a life of piety and bliss.

This scene shows Shiva standing on the right with his right hand just holding Meenakshi's right hand while Vishnu on the left is pouring the *kannikadanam* water out of a pot. Behind the wedding group is sculptured a beautiful decorative tree. This is perhaps the *karpaga Vriksham* presented to Meenakshi by Indran during her *digvijayam*. The expression on the three principal parties to the happy event is most beautifully rendered and one must note especially the shy face of Meenakshi which has yet an expressive smile. There is contentment and fulfillment in her face.

Tripurantakamurthi

One of the main valorous acts of *Shiva* is the destruction of the Three Cities by burning them referred to as *Tirupura Dahanam*. There are a number of sculptures relating to Tripurantakamurthi in the temple. An identical sculpture like the one in the Kambattadi Mandapam just referred to is in the Pudu Mandapam. The image refers to the destruction of the abodes of the three sons of Tarakasurar. Though the story is given in the *Kama Parvam* of the Mahabharatam, it is stated to be based on much older accounts in the *Samhitais* and *Brahmanams*. No less than eight forms of Tripurantakamurthi are described. The sculpture in the Kambatthadi Mandapam shows Shiva driving a chariot. His right foot rests on a part of the chariot and the left leg is planted in the front. Brahma is the charioteer. Vishnu is the arrow, Agni its barb, Yaman its feather, the Vedas make the bow and Savithri its bow-string. The whole figure looks more like a goldsmith's work rather than a stone mason's, its vigour and expression are remarkable. It is full of life. The arrow-head has the figure of Vishnu very intricately carved on such a small scale.

Kalasamhara Murthi

Kaalari is the vanquisher of Death- Kala samharamurthi. The defeat of Death by Lord Shiva is celebrated in a touching legend and given powerful form in this aspect of Shiva. The legend tells of a sonless sage Mrikandu, to whom Shiva in answer to his prayer, offered the choice of a large number of useless sons or only one son, a singularly gifted child, who would be doomed to die at the age of sixteen. The sage asked for one remarkable son and Markandeya was born and fulfilled every expectation. When the boy learnt of his fate, he went on a pilgrimage; as he worshipped the *Linga* at Thirukkadayur temple *Kala-Yama* (God of Death)

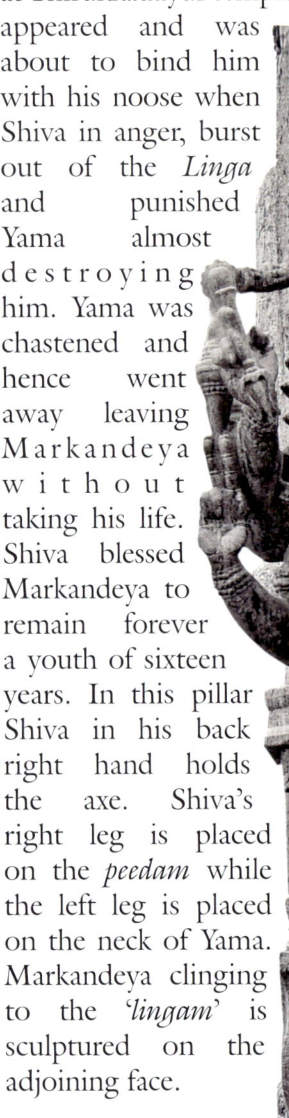

appeared and was about to bind him with his noose when Shiva in anger, burst out of the *Linga* and punished Yama almost destroying him. Yama was chastened and hence went away leaving Markandeya without taking his life. Shiva blessed Markandeya to remain forever a youth of sixteen years. In this pillar Shiva in his back right hand holds the axe. Shiva's right leg is placed on the *peedam* while the left leg is placed on the neck of Yama. Markandeya clinging to the 'lingam' is sculptured on the adjoining face.

Sukhasanar

The next pillar in the Kambatthadi Mandapam has Sukhasanar, Markandeya and Kalasamharamurthi images. The image which is labeled Sukhasanar shows Shiva with the Devi on His left. His front hands are in the *abhaya* and *varada pose*, His back right hand holds what appears to be an *Aksharamala* while his left back hand holds a Trident - *sulam*. Shiva's right leg hangs in front of the seat. Devi has two hands. In the right hand she holds a flower, the left hand is placed on the *pitham*. Devi's left leg is hanging over the seat. Also Shiva's left leg is resting on the right leg of the Devi. Perhaps this image is a form of Umamaheswara Murthi.

Pasupatha Murthy

The hunter form of Shiva, appearing before Arjuna to bless him with *Pasupatastra* is another example of Shiva's abundant grace shown to his devotees. Arjuna, the pandava prince was an ardent devotee of Shiva. He did penance to get the blessings of Shiva. Shiva appeared as a hunter and both Shiva and Arjuna rivalled each other in a boar hunt. At last Shiva showed his real form and blessed Arjuna with a mighty weapon called *Pasupatastra*. Shiva is adored as Kiratharjuna Murthi or Pasupatha Murthi in this manifestation. In this pillar Lord Shiva appears after he has presented the *'asthram'* to Arjuna who is seen on his right with the bow and arrow.

Natarajar

Shiva is Lord of Dancers, in the form of Nataraja. Shiva's dance of the cosmos; the rhythm of the movement of the sun and moon, of the earth and the wind, all pulsate in his body, the man-the microcosm who shares in and is conscious of them-is also a part of Shiva's body, the total creation. Shiva's supreme state of being in all manifestations of creation is in the dance: He is Nataraja-Lord of Dancers!

In his upper right hand, Nataraja holds the *damaru* (drum), the symbol of sound, the vibration is *Akasa* (Space), the first of the five elements which announces creation and in the palm of his upper left hand, he holds the flame – the symbol of the final conflagration of his created world. The other right hand is raised in the gesture giving freedom from fear, while the other left arm crossing the body lets its hand point to the left foot aloft, a symbol of release. The right foot is firmly planted on the infant shaped *"Apasmara Purusha"*- *Muyalakan*, the demon of forgetfulness. Shiva dances the *Ananda Tandava* in the hall of consciousness with in the heart of man.

Kama Dhahana Murthi

Kaamaari or Kama Dhahana Murthi aspect of Shiva symbolises the victory of lust by the supreme bliss. Shiva destroyed Cupid (Manmatha) with his third eye. According to mythology, the gods prayed Shiva to bless them with a child (Kumara) to destroy the troublesome demon '*Sura Padma*' but Shiva was sitting in yogic contemplation, which meant he wouldn't marry in that condition. Yet the gods wanted Shiva to marry Uma to have a son. So they thought of a plan and sent Manmatha (God of Love) to shower his flowery arrows on Shiva and cause him to love Uma. When the flowery arrows of Manmatha fell on Shiva, He opened his third eye (Agni-fire) and Manmatha was burnt to ashes. The *Kaamaari Murthi* resembles Dakshinamurthi with his third eye kept open.

Chandrasekhara Murthi

The thin crescent of the moon on the right of Shiva's Crown contributes its meaning to the significance of this form. The moon is the symbol of cyclical time and the vessel of Soma, the drink of immortality and the water of life. There is an anecdote in mythology to *Chandra* (moon) on the crown of Shiva. Daksha gave his 27 Daughters (27 birth stars) in marriage to *Chandra*. But *Chandra* was more attached to the star Rohini. This provoked jealousy among his other wives who reported the matter to their father. Daksha cursed *Chandra* to wane from his full glow. *Chandra* began to reduce and he became a crescent and prayed to Shiva to save him. Shiva in his abundant mercy, took pity on *Chandra* and wore the crescent on his crown thereby saving him from further waning. *Chandra* began to grow in brightness also. Thus the chandrasekhara form depicts the grace and the mercy of Shiva, in this manifestation. In this form in which Shiva is seen with his consort Parvathi, is known as Uma Sahitha Chandrasekarar. Shiva's forehands are in the '*abhaya*' and '*varadha*' pose. The back hands hold the axe and deer. Lord is fully decorated with ornaments.

Umasahitha Murthi or Umamaheswar

Lord Shiva is seated along with Goddess Uma/Parvathi Devi on his left. Shiva the Lord of yoga married parvathi for the sake of his devotees. The great Goddess is essentially an indivisible part of Shiva. As Uma Maheswara, this aspect shows Uma as a part of shiva's ambiance, though not of his body.

Uma Maheswara may be seen as wedded divine lovers, exalted in their embrace; they may be realized in their togetherness as *purusha* and *prakriti*, Spirit and Matter, Essence and Substance - while each level implies the other, linked by a living myth. Their co-existence subsists in the work of art. In this form Shiva is seated with Uma without Skanda in between them.

Lingodhbhavar

The *puranas* celebrate Shiva's sudden manifestation in the dark flood of cosmic *pralaya* right between two aeons. Brahma and Vishnu were the sole witnesses of the endless pillar of fire arising from the ocean. Anxious to know about the pillar, Brahma in the shape of *Hamsa* (gander) went flying upward. Vishnu in the shape of *Varaha* (wild boar) went diving into the depths of the ocean. He could not find the beginning on the pillar of fire. Vishnu admitted his failure. Brahma reported that a *pandanus* (ketaki) flower fluttered from the high, where it has been offered for worship, in corroboration that he had seen the top of the *Linga*, a lie that was to cost Brahma his head. While the two demi gods recounted their experiences, the flaming pillar split open. Both Brahma and Vishnu bowed before Shiva, whose figure in the cosmic *Linga* of flames confronted them. In this way Shiva enlightened the gods. The endless fire pillar was a sign of his presence and was worshipped on earth. Lord Shiva is carved as usual in these manifestations as emerging out of the *Lingam* with the feet hidden within the *Lingam*. He holds the axe and the deer in his back hands. The front right hand is in the '*abhaya*' pose and the front left rests on the thigh. Brahma stands in the '*anjali pose*' on the right while Vishnu in a similar pose is sculptured on the left face of the *Lingam*.

Gajamukha Anugrahar and Ravana Anugrahamurthi

Two sculptures of the episode of Ravanan under Kailasam are in the Madurai temple. One is in the Pudu Mandapam and the other, almost a copy of it, is in the Kambatthadi Mandapam. Of the two the Pudu Mandapam is more finely executed and is the better known work. The legend is how the vain Ravana is humbled by Shiva, when he tried to uproot the abode of Shiva. Shiva presses the mountain with his toe and Ravana is crushed by the Mountain and is trapped in that position. He fashions a musical instrument out of one of the heads and hands and using his own veins and nerves pleased Shiva with his music.

Chakra Dhara Murthy

This aspect of Shiva is also called Vishnu Anugrahamurthi. Once Vishnu offered one thousand lotus flowers to Shiva. As one flower fell short, he offered his own lotus eyes to Shiva. Pleased with his devotion, Shiva blessed him whith a *chakra* (discus) called '*Sudharsana Chakra*'. Thus Vishnu got the *Chakra*, and the circumstances thereof are narrated in the Shiva *puranam*. In this form Shiva is portrayed as gifting *Chakra* to Vishnu, and Shiva seated on a *peetam*. His hands hold the axe and the deer. His right hand is in '*anugraha pose*' presenting the disc and Vishnu is in standing position to the left of Shiva getting the *Chakra*. Devi Uma is also seated to the left of Shiva.

Ekapathamurthi

Ekapadamurthi is sculptured on the same side on which Rishabharudar is sculptured in the Kambattadi Mandapam. Another figure of the same image is also sculptured in the Pudu Mandapam. There is an important difference between the two representations. The sculpture in the Pudu Mandapam has Brahma issuing from the right side of Shiva and Vishnu from the left. Brahma and Vishnu have no legs as represented in some of the earlier sculptures but their front hands are held in *anjali pose* while their back hands hold their respective symbols. Brahma is represented with only one head in this sculpture. In the Kambatthadi Mandapam the Ekapathamurthi shows only Shiva. Brahman and Vishnu are not represented.

Rishbhavahanar or Rishabharudar

This is one of the most popular forms in which Shiva is worshipped in South India. The Kambatthadi sculpture shows Shiva and Parvathi seated on the back of the bull. They are represented in the same aspect as that of Uma Sahita Murthi. Shiva holds the axe and the deer in His back hands, and both the front hands are in the *abhaya* and *varada poses*. Shiva's right leg is hanging and the foot rests on a lotus. Parvathi's left foot rests in a similar manner on a lotus.

Hariharar

This form which is to the left of Ardhanari in this pillar represents another popular form of composite image with Shiva on the right and Vishnu on the left half of the image.

This aspect of Shiva is also called as Sankara Narayana. The concept of Harihara represents the unity of Shiva and Vishnu. This corresponds to that of Ardhanarishwara. In the Ardhanarishwara form the left half is occupied by Uma or Prakriti and are united with each other for the purpose of generating the universe. Uma, Durga, and Kaali are considered to be the female aspects of Vishnu.

It is related in the *Vamana Purana* that Vishnu is reported to have said to a rishi that he and Shiva are one and that in him resides Shiva also and manifested himself to the *rishi* in this dual aspect of his. In the Shiva half, the right arm is in *abhaya* pose and the back arm holds the axe. In the Vishnu half he has the conch in the left back and *'gada'* on the left arm.

Ardhanari

In this manifestation as Ardhanarishvara, the Lord whose left half is woman, reveals himself through the symbol of sexual unity as beyond the duality of Shiva and *Sakthi* (his power) for both are within him. The great God Shiva is beyond even the totality of his male-female unity. The unity of Ardhanarishwara in the sculpture is shown not as a form but as a symbol of Shiva, the ultimate reality beyond the androgynous shape of the image. It is a symbol of a higher plane than that of Uma Maheswara.

Bringi, a devotee had a view of worshipping Shiva alone. Parvathi, growing angry with Bringi, reduced him to a skeleton. He was unable to support himself in an erect position. Shiva gave him a third leg to enable him attain equilibrium. The design of Parvathi to humble Bringi thus failed. This caused great annoyance to Parvathi, who returned to do penance for obtaining a boon from Shiva. At the end of the penance Shiva granted her wish of being united with his own body. Thus is the manifestation of Shiva i.e half woman and half man form of Shiva. The right half Shiva carries axe and *'abhaya pose'* while the left Parvathi's hand is hanging down. Thus the form has three hands. A fine representation of this form is found in the pillar.

Jalandhara Vadha Murthi

Indra, also known as Devendra, since he was the king of Devas, once went to Mount Kailash to worship Shiva. But Shiva stood in a different form. Devendra asked him who he was, but there was no reply. Devendra angrily threw his *vajrayutha* on him, but it was broken to pieces. Shiva became a *Rudra* and from his sweat came out a child. He was named Jalandhara and brought up by the king of the sea (*Varuna*). Jalandhara married Brinda, the daughter of Kalanemi. He was feared by the gods. Indra ran to Shiva for help. Shiva heard his prayers and appeared as an old *rishi* before Jalandhara. Jalandhara told him that he had come to fight with Shiva. The rishi told him not to go to war with Shiva, but Jalandhara boasted of his bravery. The *rishi* drew on earth a Chakra with his finger and asked Jalandhara to take the Chakra from the earth and put it on his head. When Jalandhara took the chakra it broke him in to two pieces. Jalandhara was burnt to ashes. The Chakra was later given to Vishnu by Shiva. Here in this form Shiva holds chakra in his right hand while left hand is in Varadha pose.

Dakshina Murthi

On the pillar in the north side, on the side facing south, an important manifestation of Lord Shiva shows him seated under a banyan tree on the mount kailash engaged in yoga. This form is known as Dakshina Murthi, the Supreme Guru, who seated under a banyan tree at its root, teaches in silence, the oneness of one (innermost self) with Brahman (the ultimate reality). This knowledge is the very essence of Shiva. Shiva is not only a great yogi, but the Lord of yogis absorbed within, a totally transcendent reality which he is, but he also teaches yoga to the sages. Dakshinamurthy represents Shiva as Teacher of yoga seated in yoga posture. 'Dakshina' means south, and the name Dakshinamurthi designates the specific form of Shiva as the Lord who faces south. Dakshina also implies a gift. It implies Shiva's grace. The god shows his right hand in the gesture of imparting *Gnana* (knowledge) in silence (mounavyakya), the upper right hand holds a serpent, the lower left hand a bundle of sacrificial *kusa* grass and the upper left hand a flame.

Gaja Samhara Murthi

In the manifestation of Gaja Samahara Murthi also known as *Gajaari*, Shiva killed *Gajasura* – the elephant demon and wore the skin. In this form Shiva is shown with eight hands. Two back hands hold the hide of elephant. The other three right hands hold the axe, the trident and arrow. The three left hands hold the deer, the skull and the bow. The left leg rests on the elephant's head while the right leg instead of being bent is thrown forward to rest on the elephant's hide. Images of sages are shown in the act of adoration at the base of this form. The terrified image of Parvathi with child Skanda is carved on a side face of the pillar.

Chandesa Anugraha Murthi

The figure of Chandesa-Anugrahamurthi depicts the story of Shiva's favorite devotee – Chandesanayanar. Vicharasarma was an ardent devotee of Shiva. He started to take care of the village cattle as the current herder was not treating them properly. Under his loving care, the cattle produced lot more milk that he was left with a surplus. He started to offer the milk to Shiva. Upset with his ways, someone poisoned the mind of his father, that he was wasting the milk. His father, without enquiring the facts, tried to stop the boy's worship. Deep in his devotion, he hurled his cattle herding stick at his father, which turned into an Axe and cut off his legs. Pleased with the devotion, Shiva took him as his own and garlanded him. The carving in the Kambatthadi Mandapam shows Shiva tying the *nirmalya* garland round Vicharasarma's head and blesses him with the name Chandesa. This form consists of Shiva and Parvathi seated side by side, Chandesa bowing before them, Shiva holding the head of Chandesa with his hands and tying a flower garland (i.e the *nirmalya* garland of Shiva) round it. Chandesa is one among the five important deities in a Shiva temple and he is the 'Custodian of the temple'.

Veerabadrar

Uma was born as the daughter of Daksha Prajapathi and Shiva married her. Daksha began to hate Shiva. He wanted to perform a sacrifice without inviting Shiva, his own son in law, thereby showing disrespect to him. Dakshayani (Uma) was very unhappy about it and sought the permission of her Lord to allow her to visit her father and persuade him to invite Shiva for the sacrifice. But Shiva advised her to give up her plan because Daksha was incorrigible. But she was adamant and she came to her father's house. Daksha ill treated her and scolded Shiva. She fell in to the sacrificial fire and Shiva became furious. From his third eye manifested a *Ugra* form of Virabhadra, who destroyed the sacrifice, punished the gods present and also killed Daksha. Veerabhadra's anger caused Agni to lose hand; Indra's shoulder was injured, Brahma lost his head, Sun lost his eye and teeth, Vishnu lost his head, Yama lost his head and so on. Here in this form the following b a t t l e symbols are manifested in the right hands; the trident, the axe, and an arrow on the head of Daksha and a sword. The left hands hold the skull, the deer, the bell and the shield. Veerabhadra stands on a prostrate Daksha with his trident piercing Daksha's neck.

Bhikshatana

This Bhikshatana form depicts Shiva as the supreme naked mendicant. The sages of Dharukavana did penance but forgot the "Pravrithi Marga" (*Bakthi Marga*). Shiva wanted to teach them a lesson. He took this Bhikshatana form and made Vishnu take upon a feminine form. Both of them went to the *Dharukhavana*. The wives of the sages were enamoured by the handsome Bhikshatana (Beggar) while the sages fell in love with Mohini and forgot their penance. Bhikshatana aspect of Shiva symbolizes the mercy of Shiva. He begs our love, our devotion! and does not expect anything from us! But we have much to give up. All our evil thoughts are to be given away. Who would receive them? Shiva alone would receive them. He wants the doors of our heart to open and love poured on to his bowl. It is not so much as man seeking God as God seeking man. In this Bhikshatana form, out of the four arms, the back right arm holds the celestial drum and front right hand rests on the antelope. The back left hand has the *'Kapalam'*. Bhikshatana is dressed with only a snake coiled round him. He has bells on his leg and stands wearing sandals.

Kiratha Arjunar

The hunter form of Shiva, appearing before Arjuna to bless him with *Pasupatastra* is another example of Shiva's abundant grace shown to his devotees. Arjuna, the Pandava prince was an ardent devotee of Shiva. He did penance to get the blessings of Shiva. Shiva appeared as a hunter and both Shiva and Arjuna rivalled each other in a boar hunt. At last Shiva showed his real form and blessed Arjuna with a mighty weapon called Pasupatastra. Shiva is adored as Kiratharjuna Murthi or Pasupatha Murthi in this manifestation. In this pillar Lord Shiva is sculpted after he had presented the *'asthram'* to Arjuna who is seen on his right with the bow and arrow.

Rishabhanthakar

Dharma Devata (the presiding deity of Righteousness) feared destruction during the time of the Pralaya (great deluge) and sought refuge with Shiva taking the form of a bull. Shiva with great compassion climbed atop the bull and blessed it; taking the name of Rishabanthakamurthy. It is also said that during Shiva's annihilation of the three cities Vishnu took the form of a chariot and carried Shiva in it. In this sculpture Shiva is seen standing with his right hand resting on the bull as though blessing it. The rear arms carry an axe and a deer respectively. Lord Vishnu with his usual disc and conch is seen standing on the left and Umadevi, Shiva's consort, is seen standing on the right side.

Somaskandar

This important sculpture is also one of the best in the Kambattadi Mandapam. Shiva and Parvathi are seated in the *sukhasana* pose with a dancing figure of Skandar standing between them. Shiva holds the axe and the deer. The front right hand is in the *abhaya* pose. The front left hand is in the *simhakarna* pose. Parvathi holds a flower in her right hand and her left hand rests on the pedestal. Skandar holds a flower in each hand. The child wears a *karandamakutam*.

A fine old bronze of Somaskanda could be seen at the Thiruvappudaiyar temple on the northern bank of the *Vaigai*. The work follows classic lines and the craftsmanship shows remarkable restraint and economy. The front left hand of Shiva is in the same *simhakarna* pose as the statue in the Kambatthadi Mandapam.

A devotee in deep prayer of Lord Vinayagar at the northern side of the temple. True and unshakable faith of the devotees appear to work miracles in their lives.

Sadashivamurthy

Lord Shiva manifests himself as Sadashivamurthy with five faces, in order to teach *Shiva Agama* (Procedures for Shiva Worship) to the world. This form has five faces called Isanam, Thathpurusham, Aghoram, Sadyojatham, and Vamadevam with ten arms and fifteen eyes. In the process of liberating all living beings Lord Shiva performs five activities which go under the name *'Pancha Krithyas'*. *Mrigendra Agamam* proclaims that these five acts with five *manthras* (scriptural formulae) constitute verily the body of Shiva.

This Sadashivamurthy is seen in the *Sukhasana* pose near the *Dwarapalaka* (gate keeper) at the entrance to the first Prakara from Kambathadi Mandapam. It is a rare and beautiful sculpture which cannot be seen elsewhere.

Panchasakthi Mahadevi

Parashakthi Devi with five faces and ten arms seated in *Padmasana* pose (lotus posture) can be seen in this beautiful sculpture. The hands carry respectively the disc, conch, goad, rope, sword, shield, flag, and flower with the front two hands in the *abhaya* and *varada* poses. The figure of the Goddess has an enchanting smile in her face.

The Devi is personified as Pancha Sakthi, performing five duties and supporting the five elements. She embodies the five *Bijaksharas* of Shiva and includes the five aspects namely *Santhi* (peace), *Anandam* (Happiness), *Bhogam* (enjoyment), *Vaseekaram* (attraction), and *Karunai* (compassion) of the Lord. This image can be seen near the entrance to the first Prakara near the *Dwarapalaka* (gatekeeper).

The finer points in a sculpture can be noticed by observing this set of toes. The projecting nails on the toes are true to life reinforcing the fine workmanship of the sculptor

The imposing figure of goddess Kali instills awe and admiration in the devotee who has to but stand dumb with folded hands before the deity. Besides this more than life sculpture one can notice similar enormous figures of grand proportion; those of Urdhva Thandavar, Aghora Veerabadrar, Agni Veerabhadrar that arrest one's attention with their shear presence. These intrinsic artistic details are worth studying and appreciating.

Kali

The figure of Kaali is situated in the southern portion of the eastern side of the Kambathadi Mandapam. She is ten armed and has a flaming hair plaits and in the four right arms she holds the trident, an arrow, a tool and an urn. In the four left arms Kaali holds the skull, the bow, the noose and the bolt. The left foot of Kali rests on a gnome who is seen supporting it.

Urdhva Thandavar

The sculpture of Urdhva Thandavar is found in the southern portion of the easternside of the Kambathadi Mandapam. It represents one of the dancing forms of Shiva. This mode of dancing in which Shiva lifted His right leg straight up to the level of His head refers to a contest between Him and Kali as to who was the better dancer. As Kali danced equally well in all the forms of dancing, Shiva finally began the Urdhva Thandavam which, of course, Kali, in her modesty, could not perform. In this manifestation, out of His ten arms, five left hands hold fire, deer, arrow, shield and bell; five right hands hold the drum, the axe, sword, bow and *Abhaya* pose. *Apasmaram* (Muyalakan) is lying below the left foot of Shiva. Karaikal Ammayar is sculptured on the right side of His foot. On the left side Nandhi is sculptured with *kuta muzha* instrument.

Aghora Virabhadrar

The Aghora Virabhadrar image is situated in the northern portion of the eastern side of the Kambatthadi Mandapam. It is a noble piece of sculpture full of action in every part and with a most expressive face. It is ten-armed and has a *jatamakutam* with a *lingam* in its centre as is usual with Virabhadrar figures. Stylized flames arise out of the head. It is a fully ornamented figure. In the five right arms the following symbols are seen: a sword piercing Dakshan, an arm lifting an arrow from the quiver, the axe, the trident and the drum. In the corresponding five left arms are a large shield with a carved figure, a bow, the deer, and the thunder bolt. Aghora Virabhadrar wears many garlands as described in the *agamas*.

This figure of Lord Anjaneya baring its teeth near the Kambatthadi Mandapam is finding increasing importance among the visiting devotees due to the belief that it gives strength to accomplish things. The sculptor who had the divine inspiration while sculpting this art form should be appreciated for giving sanctity to this form.

Agni Virabhadrar

Agni Virabhadrar image is as large as Aghora Virabhadrar and its fierce and vigorous action impresses every on looker. It has a flaming hair plait and a well-shaped face with flying moustaches over a smiling mouth which, however, has fangs on either side. It has eight hands and the two front hands carry a long trident which is piercing the neck of a fallen figure over whom Virabhadrar has planted his left foot. The three remaining right hands hold the celestial drum, sword and Thunder bolt. The three left hands hold the *kapalam*, the shield and the bell. Many necklaces and garlands adorn the image which is seen with sandals on its feet.

The positive vibrations of the Meenakshi Amman temple prompts foreigners to practice the rituals followed by Hindus for ages. One can see the peace and atonement in the face of the devotee with folded hands and surrendering oneself to the vibrant Goddess.

*The imposing edifice of the celebrated golden tower beam (Dwajasthambam) glows like
Sun's ray creating radiance around it causing a vibrant atmosphere*

Thousand Pillared Mandapam

The grandest part of the entire temple is this Thousand Pillar Mandapam. It can be said that no other grand structure has been made since this was built. The sheer largeness of the hall and the towering pillars make visitors gape in awe. The Thousand Pillar Madapam is a huge edifice located in the north-east corner of the Adi Street with its north and eastern side close to the outer walls of the temple. It occupies an area of 60,000 square feet. The mandapam faces south and its entrance on that side leads to a long central nave with two rows of pillars on either side of it. The east and west wings of the mandapam are fully filled with rows of pillars of which there are 985 in the mandapam. The central nave leads to a Sabhapathi shrine which is over two stages of platforms. The shrine contains a large image of Nataraja showing him dancing on top of a large *Kurma Pitham*. *Yali* pillars flank the approaches of the shrine. The shrine wall is a later addition and it is likely that the shrine was not enclosed by walls in earlier times.

An array of pillars forming a corridor like appearance with their symmetry baffles even the best of modern day engineers.

There is a beautiful shrine on the eastern wing with finely worked details on its structural members. The *jalandharar* especially is a finely sculptured piece showing two mythical beasts. The shrine is in disuse and probably has remained so, for years past. It houses a *lingam* and the image of a goddess.

The pillars in the Thousand Pillar Mandapam are beautifully sculptured with iconographic figures. The sculpturing is in a class by itself and one could easily notice the difference between them and the other sculptures else where in the temple. These reveal a wonderful sense of form and line. The group of figures on two rows of pillars at the entrance is each one a masterpiece by itself. The carvings on the first row of pillars are Angam Vettina Shiva, Kannappar, Kankalamurthi, Ariyanatha Mudali, Harischandran, Chandramathi, Kurati and Kuravan. On the second row of pillars are the following: Pandya Rajan, Thirupurari, Ganesar, Dvarapalakars, Subrahmanyar, Nagarajar and Saraswathi. On the central row of pillars are other fine sculptures of which the following are worth mentioning - Kali, Uththara, Bhima, Purusha Miruga, Vedan, Rathi. Manmatha, Aghora Virabhadrar, Mohini and Bikshatanar. On some of the plain pillars a number of legendary and iconographic figures in a low relief are carved on the facets.

The combination of bracketed beam architecturally well composed is a good example of pillars with foliated brackets spreading out like a tree. The base of the mandapam on the western side has a frieze of panels depicting scenes from the legends in low relief.

The Thousand Pillar Mandapam is reported to have been built by Ariyanatha Mudali, the great general and minister of the first four Nayakar rulers of Madurai. An equestrian statue of Ariyanatha Mudali is on one of the front pillars.

Entrance of 1000 Pillared Mandapam

Miniature figurines carved out in Ivory
shows the finesse with which the sculptor
has done this work. This form of art work
brings out the creativity that can be
witnessed in many such sculptures in the
1000 pillar mandapam

A little girl is whispering her entreaty into the ears of the
Nandi. It is believed that such an act would fulfill every
desire according to Indian Mythology

Sculptures in Thousand Pillar Mandapam

1   Lord Shiva
2   Kannappar
3   Bhikshatanar
4   Horse Rider
5   Harischandra
6   Chandramathi
7   Gypsy Woman
8   Kannappar
9   King
10   Tripurantakar
11   Dancing Ganpathy
12   Dwarapalakar
13   Lord Muruga
14   Nagaraja
15   Palace Singer
16   Uthirai
17   Queen And Servant
18   Veerabhadrar
19   Manmathan
20   Puruasa Mirugam
21   Karnan
22   Tharugavana Rishi Wife
23   Bhikshatanar
24   Arjunan
25   Beeman
26   Rathi
27   Dhakshan
28   Hunter
29   Arjunar as eunuch

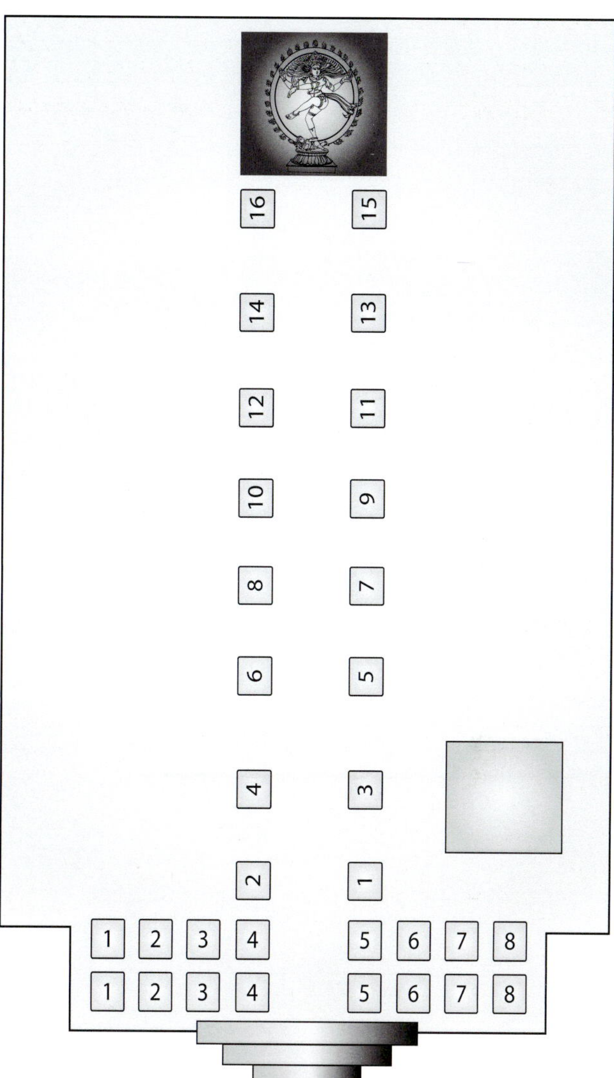

Painting of Celestial Wedding of Lord Sundareswarar during Rani Mangammal period (1690)

Lord Shiva

An episode in Thiruvilayadal Puranam describes Shiva as a sword wielding warrior who dismembers the limbs of a character called *Chithan*. In this sculpture Shiva's hands in the front hold knife and shield whereas the hands at the back hold the deer and axe. He is seen standing on *Chithan* with his feet firmly pressing the body.

Bhikshatanar

Shiva takes this form to rid the sages of *Dhaaruka* forest, of their pride. One can see how he is feeding grass to a small deer, a young one, using his right hand. The left hand holds a skull and his hands at the back are sculpted to hold the cylindrical drum and the snake together with the trident (The figure opposite this is that of Mohini, the seductress).

Kannappar

Seeing blood gushing out of the *Sivalingam's* eyes, Kannappar in a violent act of extreme devotion, searches for his eye in order to pluck it out and offer it to the Lord. This statue shows this scene. The pair of slippers worn by Kannappar has also been done with a keen sense of art.

Harischandra

A man is seen seated on a horse that is galloping on its journey ahead. This person who is holding a rod in his left hand could be construed as that of Harischandran. This reasoning is based on the statue that is found next, where one sees a woman standing with a small child held in her hands. Her face is written all over with woe and she must be Chandramathi.

Horse Attendant

This statue which is found to the left as you enter features a person deftly seated on the back of a horse. One would also get to see that the horse would have raised its front-legs and is about to charge. It is held that this statue was built by Dalavai Ariyanadha Mudhaliar who had also built this Mandapam. It is quite possible to view this as Lord Shiva's figure too. In *Thiruvilayadal*, the Lord had converted foxes into horses for the sake of Manickkavasagar and one can well imagine that this was the statue of Lord Shiva as the Horse-Man. In the pillar situated on the lower side, one can clearly see a stone carving of a fox. One can therefore conclude that the person atop the horse is none other than Lord Shiva himself, the one who converted a whole set of foxes into a whole set of horses.

Chandramathi

It is reasonable to conclude, as mentioned before that this is the statue of Chandramathi who is carrying her child Lohidhasan. If we interpret this as that of Chandramathi, then the previous statue should be that of Harischandran.

Gypsy Woman (Kurathi)

The gypsy featured in this sculpture has three children. She is holding the head of one child as she stands. On her shoulders is another that is consuming the food kept in the basket. The last, the youngest, frail and delicate, and tenderest of all, appears to be enjoying its stay in a swing formed out of a cloth that is tied to the gypsy's breast. It is feeding on the milk from its mother's breasts. The basket in her hand has been woven exquisitely and has been well represented in stone.

King

The sculpture is said to be that of a Pandya King. The erect posture and the benevolence on the face shows how great he was as a ruler. He probably ruled with a steady head, warm heart and ruthless discipline as is depicted in this figure.

Gypsy Man (Kuravan)

The Gypsy (man) is depicted sculpturally here. He holds a leash in his right hand that has a monkey tied at the other end. As he draws the monkey along, one can sense how the monkey is holding its young one in a tight embrace. The left hand has a spear. The rib-bones are prominently seen. He wears many strings of pearls around his neck and his male-hair-do enthralls the viewer.

The Elephant God Ganapathy, is seen sporting a dancing pose and is presented with his ten hands, a wonderful sight. His right leg is firmly planted on the ground and his left is bent in such a manner as to seat his powerful lady-love, *Vallabhai* - a sight which is a feast to the eyes. The *Amirtha Kalasam* is placed on Ganapathy's trunk.

Tripurantakar

Shiva's right hand has an arrow with Lord Vishnu's face at its centre. It is shown as virtually carrying fire at its edge. This statue's position is not on the chariot but is seen at the normal standing posture as it were. Just beneath the pedestal on which Shiva stands, is the memorable sight of Brahma drawing Shiva's chariot. All this when seen and read together with legends would substantiate that this is the sculpture of Tripurantakar.

Dwarapalakar

These men who are the security guards of the temple are stationed at the entrance. In the right side, Dwarapalakar is holding with *'susi' mudra* in his right hand while holding the mace in his left hand.

Lord Muruga

The image of Murugan with four arms riding his peacock is wonderful in the 1000 pillar mandapam. The spirited image is full of action and shows that He is going to war. The back hands possess *sakthi* and thunder bolt. The front right hand is held aloft as if commanding while the front left holds the reins of the peacock.

Dwarapalakar

On the other side dwarapalakar stands with one foot raised. The right hand holds the *mudra* of *'Vismaya'* while the left leg controls the figure of a serpent.

Virali - Palace Dancer

The young damsel with her hair done to perfection, possibly a dancer judged by those costumes on her body. Virali, poses with the veena in her hand. A parrot rests on her right shoulder. It is customary for the *Baanars* and *Viraliyars* to give enjoyment to the people by performing at the King's court.

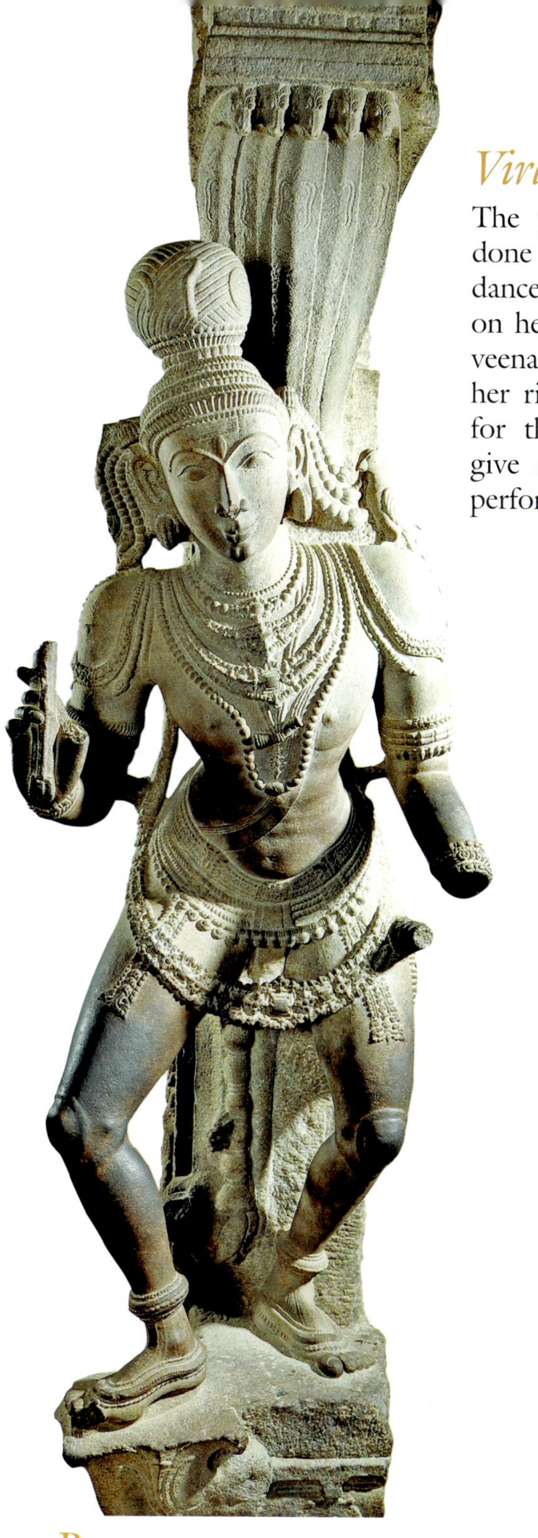

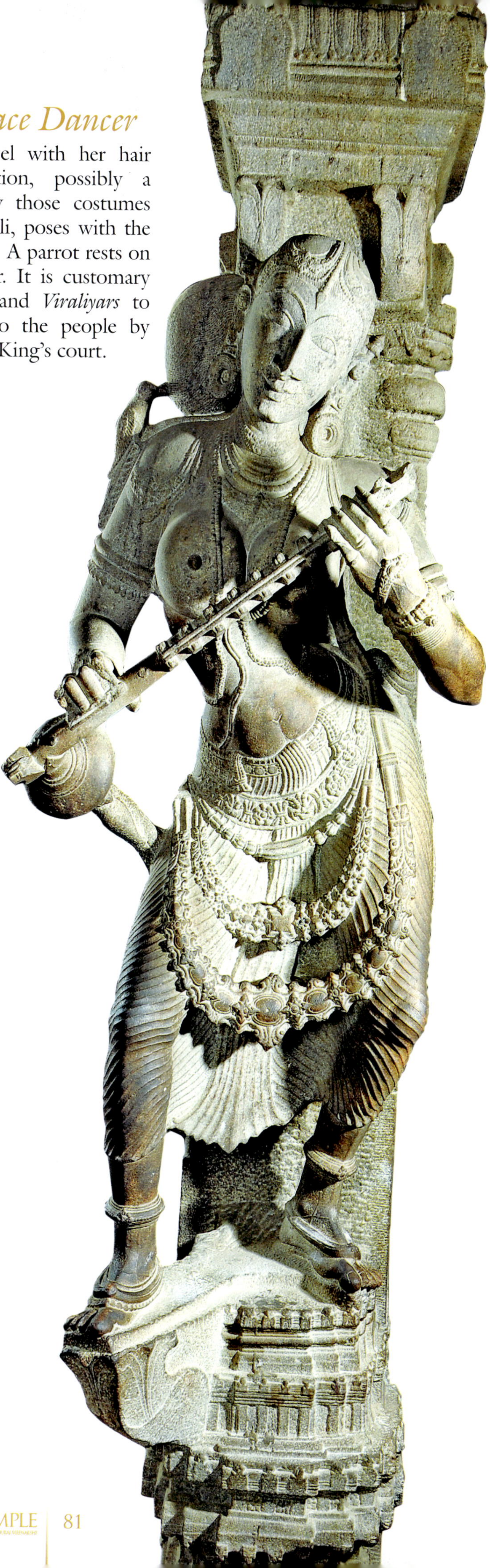

Baanan

A five-headed serpent assumes the position of a unique umbrella over the head of this statue. One cannot so easily determine whether this is the form of Baanan or someone else. The left hand unfortunately is in a broken condition and what had been held in his right hand has also met with the same fate. A parrot is perched on his left shoulder. Judging from the next statue that represents Virali, this may represent Baanan - the palace singer.

Uthirai

The statue shown standing opposite the dance guru Arjuna as a transgender (in the story of Mahabaratha), is Utharai, his disciple. As she dances she is seen holding the tassel at the end of her neatly braided long hair, with elegance. One would keep staring at this figure for the sheer engaging beauty of its crown, the jewelry and the lovely dress.

Queen And Servant

One is unable to know exactly the historical significance of this statue. The lady seated on the back of the servant looks like the Princess. It appears that she is commanding the servant to "double up", by waving her right hand in that manner. The right hand of the servant has been damaged at the wrist.

Veerabhadrar

Veerabhadrar, the one who destroyed the pride and pomp of Dakshan, is shown here with his right leg on Dakshan's head. Next to him is Nandi worshipping Veerabhadrar. Veerabhadrar's face and eyes express a state of heightened and explicit anger and under his feet is laid a garland of skulls.

This is the God of Love - Manmathan. His right hand holds the sugarcane - Cupid's flowery arrow - which has been damaged - probably by invaders.

Karnan

Karnan and Arjunan are taking sides and are shown on pillars opposite one another. Kunthi Devi had obtained Karnan's word that he would not deploy the invincible weapon, *Nagasthiram* more than once on Arjuna. This statue shows Karna with this weapon (*NagaKanai*) in his hand.

Purasha Mirugam

This character, Purusha Mirugam, is associated with the epic, Mahabharatha. When the Pandavas performed the holy sacrifice, an act of propitiation, Purusha Mirugam helped them by providing milk that quenched their thirst. This is a double-figure - it is a man above the hip and an animal below. This too holds the mace in its right hand.

Mohini

Lord Mahavishnu taking on the role of Mohini is shown here as an example of beauty and is standing in a pretty and stylish manner. The sages watching her get intoxicated by the beauty appearing before them.

Bhikshatanar

In the form depicted of Bhishatanar, the hands towards the back are sculpted to hold the cylindrical drum and the snake together with the trident. The wives of the troubled sages are shown nearby. On the left side, a *Bhoothagana* is holding the huge metal vessel (*gangaalam*) on its head.

Arjunan

Arjunan is raring to go and is holding the sword in his right hand. Regrettably, the left hand is broken, and one is not in a position to say what weapon was held by this hand.

Bhiman

Here is Bhima, the younger brother of Dharman of the Pancha Pandavas, shown with the well-curved and groomed moustache and holding aloft his mace (*Gadhai*) in his right hand.

Rathi

The ineffably beautiful wife of Manmathan, Rathi is gracefully seated on the swan and has a brisk appearance. She holds a bouquet in her hand and lovely women around her are fanning her smilingly. Should one mention that the winsome sight of the Goddess of Love, Rathi with her graceful demeanor along with Manmathan, would draw viewers and capture their attention?

Dhakshan

Dakshan is holding his sword in his right hand and the depiction shown here is the one where he is confronting Veerabhadrar. His face is a picture of pitched anger. His left hand has been damaged and perhaps, it had carried the shield.

Arjunan in feminine Form

In the Mahabharatha, a curse befell on the Pandavas and Arjuna had to assume the role of a eunuch named Brihannalai. He taught dance to King Virata's daughter, Utharai. This is displayed here where Arjuna exists as a transgender with a masculine moustache seen prominently on his face and all other features of his are feminine. His/Her long hair is braided delectably.

Hunter

The hunter is seen here with the bow on his shoulders. As he stands, both his hands have disappeared from their middle portions, a testimony to the hand work of Mailk Kafur - the invader.

Musical Pillar

In the south eastern corner of this Mandapam one can see the pillars endowed with musical properties. Those musical pillars give the seven *swaras* (notes) that form the very basis of music - Sa Ri Ga Ma Pa Dha Ni. If pillars of stone can produce such varied notes on tapping, it only shows the mastery of the sculptor, his complete involvement and skill in such a creative pursuit.

An old lady lost in her thoughts while praying before the gopuram with folded hands. It is said that the gopuram darshan and worship is considered to be equal to worshiping the Goddess.

Pudu Mandapam

One of the most publicised edifices in the Madurai temple is the Pudu Mandapam built by Thirumalai Nayakar between 1626 and 1633 A.D. This is a large corridor measuring 34,650 square feet and is axially in front of the east *gopuram*. Along the length of it is a central nave with an aisle on either side of it provided by four rows of pillars. The mandapam belongs to the Madurai period of architecture and has all the four styles of pillars, the decorative compound type, the *yali* type, the iconographic type and the portrait type pillars. The whole mandapam is the high watermark of medieval building craft. At the western end, that is, at the end next to the east *gopuram*, there is a platform with a canopy supported by a number of polished black stone pillars. This canopied mandapam is known as the Vasantha Mandapam to which the images of Meenakshi and Sundareshwarar are brought on certain festival occasions. Ten statues of Nayaka rulers of Madurai from Viswanathar to Thirumalai Nayakar are on five pillars on either side in the centre of the nave. Equestrian and *yali* pillars are on the outer pillars at the entrance on the east and west side. These areas also have many pillars with iconographic figures. The whole corridor is an imposing structure revealing very good planning and excellent execution.

Sculptures of Pudu Mandapam

1 Ravananugrahar
2 Tripura Samharar
3 Kali
4 Kalyanasundarar
5 Brahma
6 Indra
7 Ardhanari
8 Urdhva Tandavar
9 Sankara Narayanar
10 Athikaranandhi
11 Initiating Black Bird
12 Siddhar feeding Stone Elephant
13 Patanjali
14 Vyagrapadar
15 Dwarapalakar
16 Thadatakai
17 Chandran
18 Sundareshwarar feeding Piglets
19 Sundareshwarar feeding Lambs
20 Surya
21 Ekapather
22 Gaja Samharar
23 Horse Rider
24 Yali

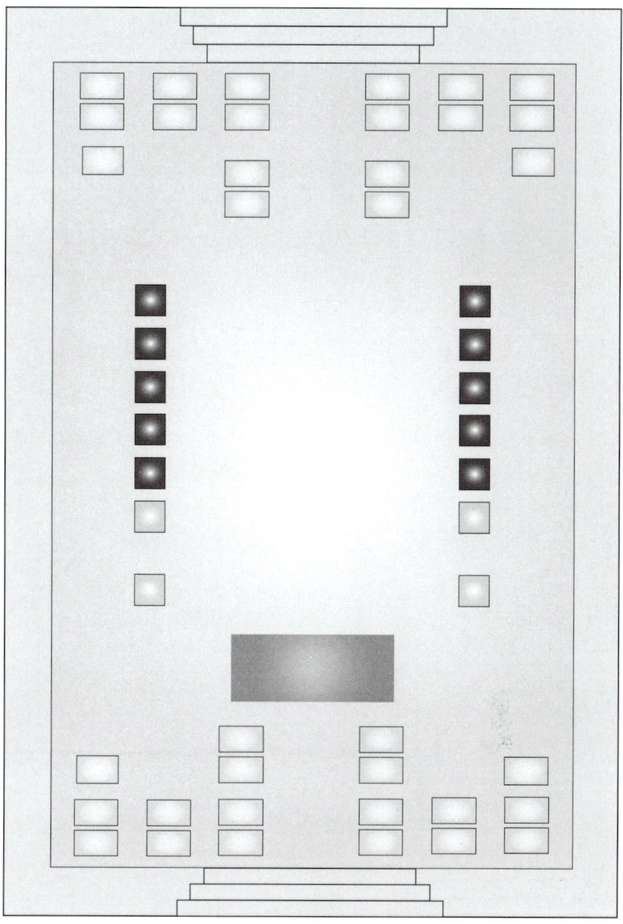

Vast hall that housed the large festivities during the Tirumalai Nayakar period.

Pudhu Mandapam
(New Mandapam)

In order to celebrate festivals held during the summer season, the Kings of the Vijayanagara dynasty and those belonging to the Nayakars, built spacious *mandapams* within the precincts of the temples. These would be on a raised ground at its centre and have depth all around the sides. In these *mandapams* the moat like forms on the sides would be filled with water, resulting in the blowing in of a comforting cool breeze that would please the visitors. Those *mandapams* with such cooling facility meant for enjoyment during the summer season were called Vasantha Mandapams.

At these *Mandapams* sculptures relating to the Puranic period, the statues of Nayakars, warriors on horseback would be the presenting order.

The presiding deity would be put up on the granite stage during festival periods. At the centre of the *Mandapam* one can witness the statues of the ten Kings of the Nayakar period in the following order.

1.   Viswanatha Nayakar
2.   Kumara Krishnappa Nayakar
3.   Periya Veerappa Nayakar

Kumara Krishnappa Nayakar

Viswanatha Nayakar

4.   Krishnappa Nayakar

5.   Lingama Nayakar

6.   Krishnappa Nayakar (II)

7.   Kasthuri Rangappa Nayakar

8.   Muthu Krishnappa Nayakar

9.   Muthu Veerappa Nayakar

10.   Thirumalai Nayakar

Thirumalai Nayakar is seen with his four wives and Kasthuri Rangappa Nayakar is seen with two.

This New Mandapam was completed in 1635. In the same year the ten day festival (Vasantha Vizha) was celebrated in a grand manner. For this festival, *Nayakar* himself wore the Parivattam (cloth tied round the head of a person in a temple as a mark of honour) around his head and even today during Vasantha Vizha Naicker's statue is decorated by tying the Parivattam around his head.

Most of the images seen in this mandapam bear a remarkable relationship with Lord Shiva's 64 forms and with those appearing in *Thiruvilayadal Puranam* (Divine Sport).

Periya Veerappa Nayakar

Thirmalai Nayakar

Krishnappa Nayakar

Lingama Nayakar

Krishnappa Nayakar (II)

Kasthuri Rangappa Nayakar

Muthu Krishnappa Nayakar

Muthu Veerappa Nayakar

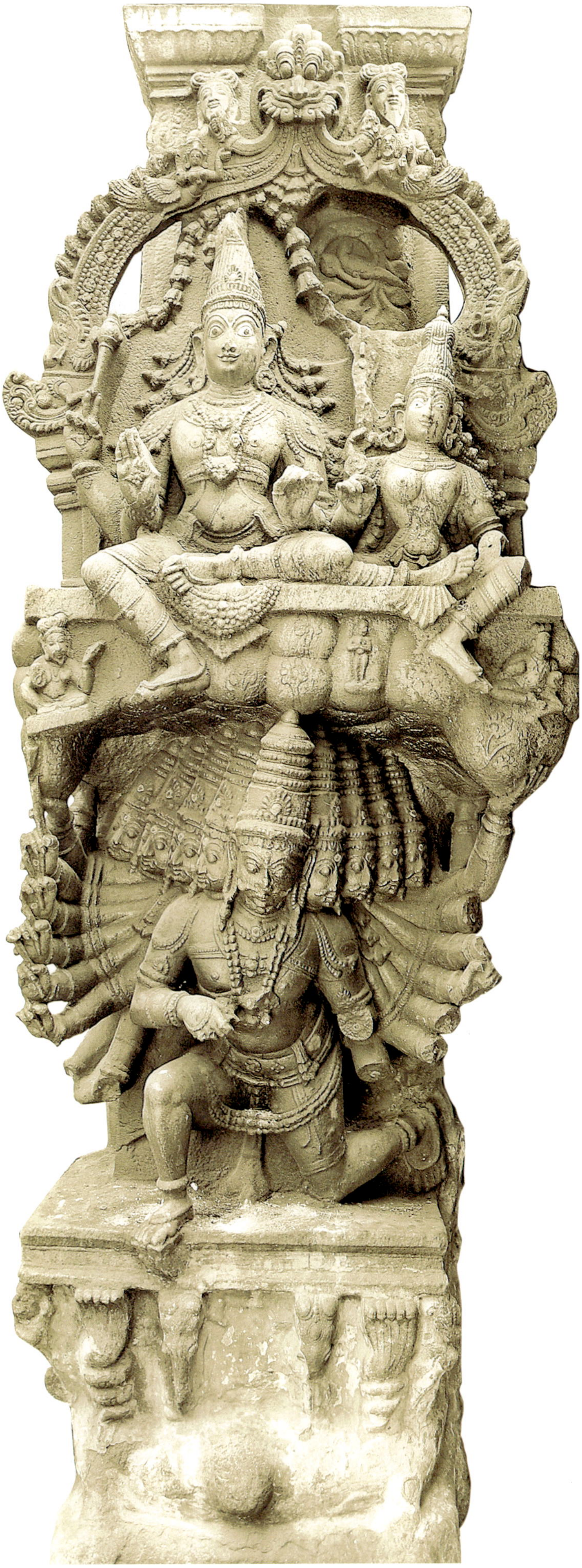

Raavana Anugrahamoorthy

Ravanan is lifting the mountain of Kailash and Lord Shiva with his consort Umadevi is seen seated atop the mountain.

Thripurantakar

Shiva's right hand has an arrow with Lord Vishnu's face at its centre. It is shown as virtually carrying fire at its edge. This statue's position is not on the chariot but is seen at the normal standing level as it were. Just beneath the pedestal on which Shiva stands, is the memorable sight of Brahma drawing Shiva's chariot. All this when seen and read together with legend, would substantiate that this is the sculpture of Thripurantakar.

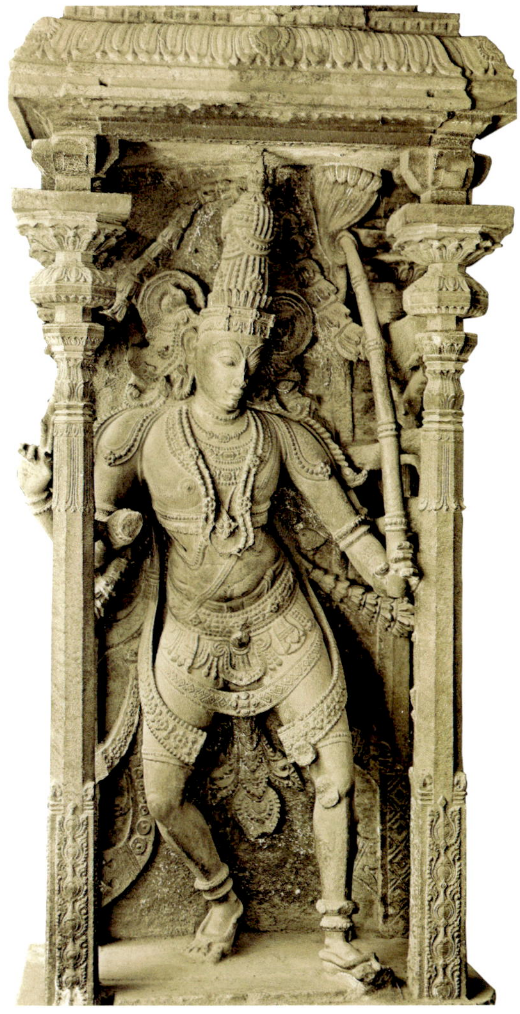

Kali

Here is Kaali seen with her eight hands and depicted to exhibit the whole intensity of her fury. It is a production on stone that is both lovely and artful. She carries in her right hands the trident, the arrow, the elephant goad, the huge knife whereas her left hands hold the bow, the skull, the urn and the shield. The biggest figures in the Pudhu Mandapam are those of Kali and Urdhva Tandavar Murthy.

Meenakshi Kalyanam

Mahavishnu preforms the marriage ceremony by pouring water to solemnize the marriage of Meenakshi and Sundareshwarar as they are seen in this statue.

Brahman

Brahama is seen here three-faced, with his four hands. One face could be seen from the rear side. Both hands on the back side hold the flagon (*kamandalam*) and the sacred beaded-string used for meditation and of the two hands in the front, one is offering protection and the other carries the holy book. This is situated near Kalyanasundarar.

Urdhva Tandavar

This statue which is enormous in its size, seen with *thiruvasi*, (with the crescent) has many fine sculptures added to it. The left leg is on *muyalakan* and the right leg is lifted heavenwards and the eight hands hold the small hand-drum, raw- fire, a shield, flag, an axe-like weapon, the knife, the trident handle – all of these in that order. On either side of this figure one sees Lord Vishnu and Brahman playing instruments. *Nandidevar* is playing on the drum in the shape of a pot, goblins around blow the conch and the others around include Karaikal Ammayar (among other saints).

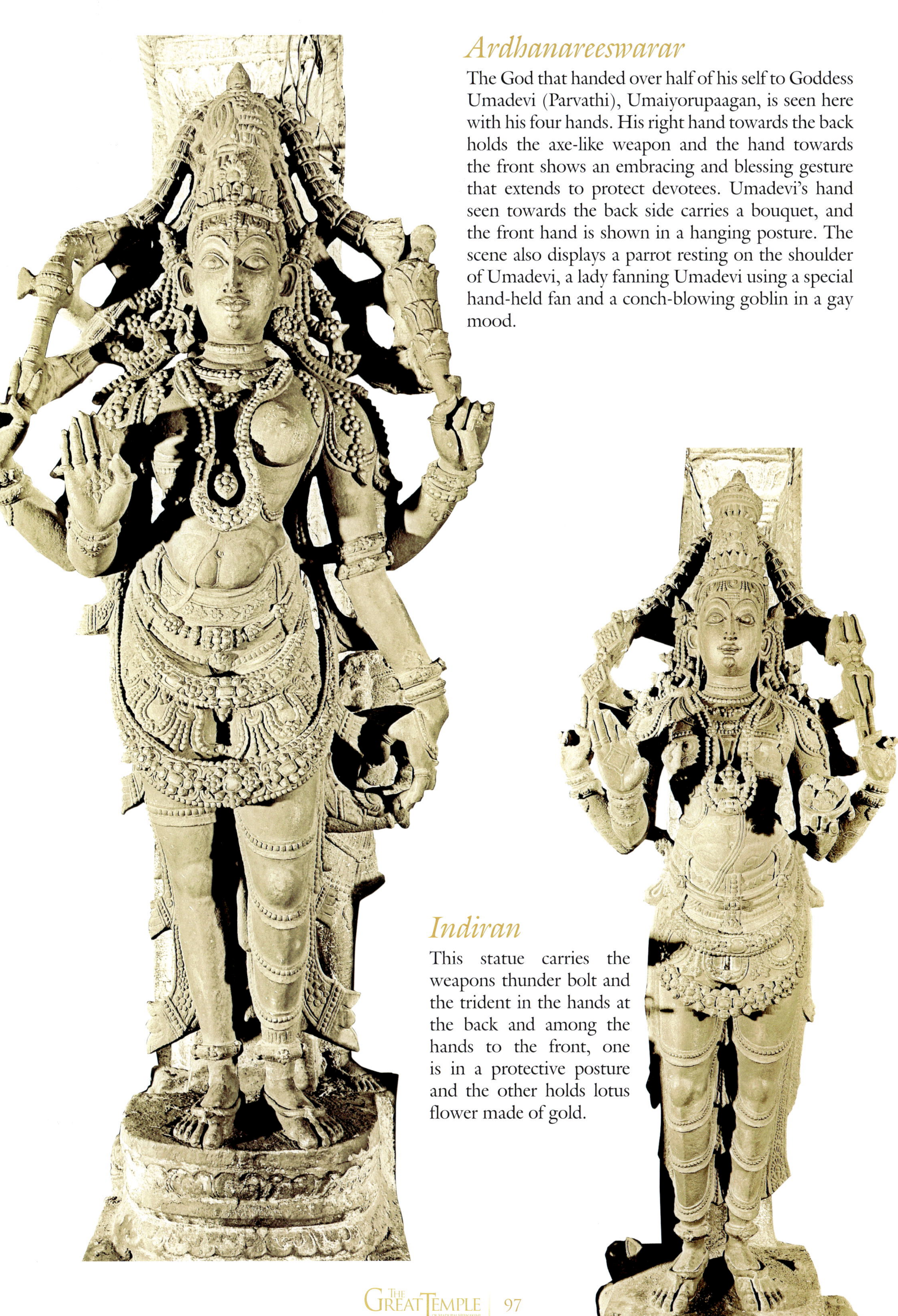

Ardhanareeswarar

The God that handed over half of his self to Goddess Umadevi (Parvathi), Umaiyorupaagan, is seen here with his four hands. His right hand towards the back holds the axe-like weapon and the hand towards the front shows an embracing and blessing gesture that extends to protect devotees. Umadevi's hand seen towards the back side carries a bouquet, and the front hand is shown in a hanging posture. The scene also displays a parrot resting on the shoulder of Umadevi, a lady fanning Umadevi using a special hand-held fan and a conch-blowing goblin in a gay mood.

Indiran

This statue carries the weapons thunder bolt and the trident in the hands at the back and among the hands to the front, one is in a protective posture and the other holds lotus flower made of gold.

Blessings to the Black-sparrow

This statue has its connection with the story where the black sparrow is blessed to learn from the Lord - a story that occurs in *Thirvilayadal Puranam* (Divine Sport). In spite of having done many good deeds, as a punishment for doing a lone despicable act, a person is cursed to be born as a black sparrow. In order to escape the persecution by other bird groups, this sparrow opts to lead its life in the dense forest. A saint appears, stands under a tree and gives a sermon on the significance of Madurai – its name, the place and the sacred water it possesses. The black sparrow that was intently listening to all this reaches Madurai and circumambulates the temple for three days. Lord Shiva is more than pleased at its sincerity and worship and reveals to it the *"Mrithunjaya" mantram* (a power-packed and sacred set of words for the purpose of meditation). This causes the bird to become the leader among birds, attain name and fame; and God further assigns the name of *"Valiyan"* to it and blesses it. This sculpture shows Lord Shiva with his four hands, with the deer, the spear, the left hand in the front holding the black sparrow itself and the right hand showing the sign of enlightenment.

Adhigaara Nandhi

In a venerable standing posture, presenting all four hands - where the hands at the back hold a deer and a tomahawk and the hands at the front being brought together in a worshipful mode - is the statue of Adhigaara Nandhi.

Here is a piece of work that talks of another incident mentioned in *Thirvilayadal Puranam* (Divine Sport). The Lord appears as a mystic having a phenomenal strength and wins the acclaim of the people who get attracted by his tricks and performances. The Pandya King meets him and gives him a poser: " If you are an all powerful man, can you make this elephant made of stone that "lives" here eat sugarcane?". The elephant comes alive, eats the sugarcane thus offered and is emboldened to snatch the diamond chain worn by the King. And as the men in-charge of security make an attempt to negotiate the elephant, the mere word "stop" from this mystic leaves the men, in a stand still position. The King realises the greatness of this mystic, then falls at his feet and pleads for pardon. At the wink of the mystics eye, the men become normal, the elephant hands over the King's chain through its trunk and re-assumes its position as a statue in stone. Here Lord Shiva is seen as the mystic with two hands. He is wearing the crown on his head, holds the sugarcane in his left hand and the image of the elephant is close to his right hand.

Thadathagai Piraatti

Here Thadathagai Piraatti is shown as one who ruled Madurai and undertook her expedition as a conqueror - her target being all directions. She is seen riding a chariot and is shown with her characteristic three breasts holding the symbol of Queenship in her right hand. She is surrounded by Shakthi's warriors with their swords drawn out, who seem to be moving in a procession as it were.

Dwarapalakar

These men who are the security guards stationed at the entrance are shown with the "*Vismaya*" and "*Susi*" *mudhras*.

Sundareswarar

Thadathagai went on her venture, waged battles and won even supernatural beings (Devas), and turned her attention to Lord Shiva who was on Mount Kailash and invited him for a battle. This statue shows Lord Shiva in a ready-to-go state. His hands are holding the deer, the tomahawk, the bow with its arrows and is in the form of *Thribanga*,(three bends) putting one foot forward and is in the *Aaalida* move as he is shown here.

Dwarapalakar

These men who are the security guards stationed at the entrance are shown with the *"Vismaya"* and *"Susi" mudhras.*

The Lord who fed the piglets

Sugalan and Sugalai had given birth to 12 children, who were - thanks to an evil curse from a saint - born as piglets. When the Pandya King came hunting to the forest, he could see these piglets in extreme hunger as their parents were dying. At this hour Lord Shiva came down to the earth as the mother pig and nursed these piglets. As a consequence , the pigs became entities in double states, retaining the body of a human being and had a face that resembled a pig. This sculpture shows The Lord taking the form (*avathara*) of the mother pig and in a standing posture, is caressingly holding six piglets, three on each side. The piglets are shown being nursed and consuming milk from its mother's udder. Further two piglets are shown under the feet of the Lord and two more by the side. Lord Shiva who became a pig himself has in his hands the spear and a deer. This anecdote, where the Lord took mercy on these pigs, though they were mere animals, became its mother and showered mercy on them, is a part of the *Thiruvilayadal Puranam* (Divine Sport).

Pathanjali

Pathanjali and Vyagrapathar are those privileged men who were fortunate enough to witness the dance of Lord Shiva. They had come for the holy marriage of Meenakshi Ammai, and were insistent that they would consume food only after enjoying the dance of the Master of Dancers. The Lord acceded to their wish and hence *Velliyambalam* gained in fame. One can see here that a snake has taken the form of an umbrella that is held over Pathanjali's head.

The young ones of the deer being fed by a tigress

This particular statue is according to the memorable work of Perumpatrappuliyur Nambi's *Thiruvilayadal Puranam*. A deer that had given birth, ran hither and thither to quench its thirst and finally located a pond and drank water from it. During this act, hunters' arrows consumed the deer and the poor young ones, now left motherless, could not bear the hunger. Lord Shiva seeing the plight of these young ones, sends a tigress to nurse them. Here The Lord is again shown in a standing posture with his hands at the back holding the spear and the deer. His right hand held in the front is holding those young ones and his left hand provides space for the tigress. There are a few young deer close to his feet also.

Vyagrapathar

Vyagrapatha is one of those privileged who were fortunate enough to witness the dance of Lord Shiva. During the wedding of Meenakshiammai, the Lord acceded to their wish and performed the ritual dance. The saint Vyagrapathar is depicted here with the nails on his feet shown as that of a tiger. (*Vyagra* meaning tiger and *pada* meaning foot)

Ekapaadha Thrimurthy

This is a unique statue where Lord Shiva is seen resting on a single leg. Up to the hip on the right it is Brahma's figure and to the left it is the figure resembling the half-shape of Lord Vishnu. Vishnu and Brahma are seen in the postures of dignified obeisance. Lord Shiva's hands towards the back side carry the spear and the deer and in the front side are seen with the protective and Varadha signs *(mudhras)*. *The Varadha mudhra* (pose) is customarily used whenever a blessing is being offered. On either side one can see sages worshipping the Lord.

Gajasamhara Murthy

When the sages of Dharukavanam were performing the Yagna (*Aabisara Yagna*) an elephant caused a disturbance. Lord Shiva split the elephant, tore its skin and wore it around him, exhibiting valor of a high order. This statue shows him in this mood with eight performing hands. A lovely piece of work indeed!

Sooriyan (Sun God)

On the head portion of this sculpture, that of *Sooriyan* (the Sun God), is Orb (*Prabhai*). *Sooriyan* is shown atop a chariot where the hands at the back are shown carrying lotus flowers. Of the hands in the front, one shows the protective bearing and the other is gracefully placed on the hip.

Warriors on horse-back

On the western side of the Pudhu Mandapam, there are sculptures of four warriors on horse-back and on the eastern side are two such warriors. In this total of six, we can observe charge given by these warriors to the horses to gallop faster. And as it proceeds, we also see statues where these warriors take on the tigers running around, tearing them apart with their spears. The *Mandapams* built by the Vijayanagara-Nayakar combinations have such warrior figures aplenty.

Yalis

The lion, the elephant and the crocodile – a unique combination of these, forms the Yali. The New Mandapam has ten Yalis. The Mandapam as a whole has such lovely art pieces, in abundance.

Prayers being offered with heart and soul.

Carrying Earth in return for *Pittu* (Sweet Rice Flour)

Once there was a great flood in Vaigai River. Flood waters threatened to enter Madurai breaking the bunds. The king ordered that one male member should volunteer from each family to reinforce the bunds with earth. Vandhi was an old lady with no issues, herself eke outing her livelihood by sale of *Pittu* (sweet rice flour). Seeing her sorry plight the Lord himself offered to represent her in return for a handful of *Pittu* (sweet rice flour). However the Lord turned laborer, without performing his duty; whiled away lazily. When the irate soldiers lashed the labourer, that lash landed on every one's back including the king. The king realized that this must be one of the divine sports of Somasundarar and praised his compassion. This event is celebrated on the ninth day festival of *Avani Moolam* when the Lord is decorated in the fashion of a laborer carrying earth for Vandhi.

Other Mandapams

Ashtasakthi Mandapam

One of the most beautiful of the entrances to the Madurai temple is the Ashtasakti Mandapam which is axially in line with the Meenakshi shrine. This mandapam is actually the main entrance to the temple in the present day. Its frontage is formed of a high portal with a large tower over it and two smaller towers on either side of it on top of the two side walls. Two stucco figures of Ganesha and Shanmukhar are on the upper level on the side walls.

Proceeding inside one finds a colonnade of two rows of pillars over which is an arched roof. The front row of pillars have the figures of the eight *Ashtasaktis* after whom the mandapam is named. On four of the second row of pillars on either side there are four statues of Nayakar rulers. Behind this second row of pillars are shops dealing in a variety of articles. Panels of stucco figures with painted background are now in the cloister that was once below the arched roof. The ceiling of the roof is decorated with floral designs enclosing five *yantram* designs peculiar to *Devi*. At the western end are two fine stone figures of Maha Ganapathi and Shanmukhar and these perhaps served as the model for the stucco figures on the front wall of the entrance.

Vaishnavi

Paintings using rich and bright colors depicting the life of Meenakshi Amman on the roof of the mandapam

Yagnarupini

Mahalakshmi

Rowthiri

Maheswari

Koumari

Shyamala

Manonmani

Mudhalipillai Mandapam

Mudhali Pillai Mandapam which lies between the Chithira Gopuram and the north-east corner of the Golden Lily Pond is popularly known as the Dark Mandapam for it is enclosed by walls and very little light reaches it. It contains six sculptured pillars of which five relate to the Bhikshatanar - Mohini legend. Statues of Bhikshatanar, Saints of the Dharukavanam and wives of saints. Mythology has it that Lord Shiva took the form of Bhikshatanar to preach to the *Munivars* of Dharukavanam. The Statues of Saints, Mohini and Kadanthai Mudaliar are seen at the southern side of the mandapam.

Muthupillai Mandapam was built by
Kadathai Mudaliar in 1613 AD

Veda Mandapam

The Mandapam built next to the Ashtasakthi Mandapam is called the Veda Mandapam. Both on the left and right side of this Mandapam one can see those magnificent 6 foot statues of the hunter and his female counterpart - indeed a lovely and eye-catching sight.

This hunter and the woman really represent Shiva and Parvathi. The woman holds the trident (slightly damaged though) in her hands and is in possession of a skull too. The kind of dress draped around the breasts makes this statue unquestionably that of a Goddess. Whenever women characters are portrayed in stone, this particular garb is shown always around the breasts, especially when it applies to those residing in heaven. As what has been sculpted here is that of a Goddess, this particular dress, the *Kachchai*, is shown around her breasts. We also find powerful instruments of enormous strength nearby. The figure over the head is that of the serpent. The hunter is seen in the company of a bird and a monkey and on his shoulders he carries a snake. This proves beyond doubt that here is the statue of Lord Shiva

Killikoondu Mandapam built by Abisheka Pandaram in 1623 AD seen on western side of Golden Lily Pond..

Karnan

Dharman

Kilikikoodu Mandapam

Kilikkoodu Mandapam (parrot cage like pillared hall), also known as Sangili Mandapam (chain hall) is where during the festival days, youngsters play *kolattam* (dance with sticks). Colored ropes are suspended from a central point in the roof and children dance with sticks holding on to the ropes. The ropes twist and untwist around each other forming a chain; hence the name Sangili Mandapam to this pillared hall.

In this hall, sculptures are seen in juxtaposition to each other with the five Pandavas carrying bow and arrow except Bhima. Sahadeva is seen with a bow as well as a raised sword in the right hand. Arjuna is seen sporting a beard, perhaps to signify his penance in the forest for obtaining the Pasupatha missile. The sculpture opposite Arjuna carries a *Nagakkanai* (serpent missile). This must be Karna who was beseeched by his mother Kunti, not to use the serpent missile more than once on Arjuna. In the sculptures depicting Vali and Sugreeva (the monkey chieftains of Ramayana) *Vali* is seen larger in size than Sugreeva, with both ready for a wrestling bout. Vali is seen beating his chest and Sugreeva tapping his thigh typical of wrestlers of great prowess. In the adjoining pillar a hunter and a dancing girl are sculpted with great artistry. There is also a figure of half man-half animal in the neighboring pillar reminding us of a Mahabharata episode.

Sahadevan

Nagulan

Beeman

In the ceiling of the Kilikkoodu Mandapam, along the periphery in a circle, we see the sixty four divine sports of Lord Sundareshwarar in small sizes but exquisitely portrayed. In this mandapam adjacent to the gate to the kitchen, one can see the historic grinding stone used by Moorthy Nayanar, one of the sixty three *Nayanars* (saivite savants of Periya Puranam). Moorthy Nayanar, a staunch devotee of Shiva used to offer sandal wood paste to the Lord daily without fail. When Madurai was overtaken by a Jain king, a decree was proclaimed that no sandal wood should be provided to Moorthy Nayanar. Unable to bear the thought of failing in his sacred duty, he started grinding his elbow against this stone. The Lord instantly appeared before him, blessed him and installed him as the king of Madurai.

The colorful murals on the ceiling of the Kilikoondu mandapam are a treat to watch

Purushamirugam

Vali

Sugrivan

To the left of the gate leading to the sanctum of Meenakshi Amman from the Kilikkoodu Mandapam one can see on the left side the shrine of Siddhi Vinayaka. On the right side one can see Koodal Kumaran's shrine. Arunagirinathar has sung the praise of *Koodal Kumaran* in his Thiruppugazh.

Skillful sculpture that shows a ring going through another set of rings - all done in a single piece of stone

Painstaking stone craft in sculpting as seen in the ball inside the mouth of yali - all crafted in a single piece stone work

Dancer

Hunter

Gate Keeper

Veera Vasantharaya Mandapam

The Veera Vasantharaya Mandapam is immediately situated to the west of the east *gopuram* and is almost as long as the Pudu Mandapam which is on the other side of the east *gopuram*. The Vira Vasantharaya Mandapam has a long central nave and an aisle on each side of it and its tall and slender compound pillars which are variously patterned support a high ceiling that is roofed with long slabs. At the entrance to the mandapam on the eastern side are the figures of Rudhrar, Rudhrakali, Kaali and Kalasamkaramurthi sculptured on pillars. On the ceiling is a large carved panel with colorful paintings and lotus medal lions. According to the *Thiruppani Vivaram*, Muthu Virappar, the brother, of Thirumalai Nayakar I, is reputed to have built this mandapam in 1611 A.D.

Nagara Mandapam

Facing the Ashtasakthi Mandapam is the *Nagara Mandapam or Aagaya Mandapam* which is stated to have been built by Kamattam Achutanararayan, a minister of Mangammal. This mandapam which was used for storing the *vahanams*, contains a much white-washed statue of Rani Mangammal with her grandson, similar to the one in Thirupparankundram, in one of the pillars near the entrance. It was a customary action to beat the *Nagara*, a percussion instrument atleast once in a day.

Vira Vasantharaya Mandapam situated adjacent to the East Rajagopuram was built by Muthuveerappa Nayakar in the year 1611 A.D.

Nagara mandapam situated opposite the Amman sanctum in East Chitra street was built in the year 1635 by Achutharayan, minister of Rani Mangammal.

Telescopic view of the Mandapam

The Meenakshi Nayakar Mandapam

The Meenakshi Nayakar Mandapam which leads to the Amman shrine is between the Chithira Gopuram and the Ashtasakthi Mandapam. It has six rows of pillars forming a central nave and two aisles on either side. The central nave is more than 20 feet broad. The pillars are of the square compound type as in other structures in Madurai with a bracketed capital above, composed of lions and Madurai corbels with connecting beams. The pillar shafts have delicately carved floral designs. At the western end is a huge metal arch. At the entrance to the mandapam on the east are two figures of a hunter and his wife carved on two pillars. They probably represent *Iswaran* and His Devi in this form. The two figures are almost in a similar attitude and are well sculptured with.less idealism in their features. On one of the pillars in the central nave is a diminutive figure of Meenakshi Amman as she was before she met her future consort Sundareshwarar in the course of her *digvijayam*. The ceiling of the central nave has a large carving of a *rasi chakram*. It is generally thought that Meenakshi Nayakar III, one of the ministers of Thirumalai Nayakar, built this mandapam.

The Mandapa Nayaka Mandapam

This mandapam is in the north-east corner of the Swami Sanctum's second *prakaram* and faces south. It is also called the Hundred Pillar Mandapam. It is a seven-aisled mandapam, at the end of which is Sabhapathi temple which is built over a low *adhisthanam*. The Sabhapathi temple has a large idol of Natarajar well carved in stone. In front of the shrine is a small four-pillared mandapam. The four pillars are of black polished stone and the base of the mandapam is supported by *asthagajams*. As usual images of Pathanjali and Viyaghrapadhar are found in this shrine also. The mandapam with its well-spaced pillars has a reputation as one of the most beautiful in the temple. There is a frieze over the lintel at the entrance to the shrine and its small carved figures relate to the legend of Meenakshi's marriage.

Naalvar Koil

The southern end of the Kambattadi Mandapam leads to the *Naalvar* shrine which is situated on the platform of the *prakaram*. This mandapam is stated to have been built by Krishna Virappa Nayakar about 1572 A.D. The images of Gnanasambandar, Mangayaarkarasi, Koon Pandian, Kulachiraiyar, Appar and Maanikka Vasagar are in the *Nalvar Koil*.

The rich wooden carvings and paintings that depict the Divine Sport. The sacred wedding hall to the south of *Veeravasantharayar* mandapam was built by *Vijayaranga Sokkanatha Nayakar (1706 - 1732). The golden chariot of the temple is kept in this Mandapam.*

The Kalyana Mandapam

This is a place that should not be missed under any pretext. It reflects the same grandeur that prevailed during the celestial wedding of Goddess Meenakshi. On all occasions that symbolise auspicious beginnings, be it the enactment of *Meenakshi Thirukalyanam*, festivities of the God and Goddess or for that matter any of the devotees special *puja* for the God and Goddess, the commencement takes place at this mandapam only.

The place leaves one in ecstasy after seeing the beautiful wooden carvings and the nuances in the details. The Divine Sport stories have been painted with such finesse that it needs no explanation to understand the Sport. The symmetry along the walls and the wonderful presentation on the roof speaks of the greatness of the artisans in those times.

The Kalyana Mandapam abuts the eastern wall of the Swami Sanctum's second *prakaram*. It was originally an open mandapam, but at present it is enclosed by walls on all sides except the east. It has foliated arches. The side walls of the north and south carry two huge paintings of the "Two Worlds" according to Hindu cosmology *(Kakolam and Pukolam)*. In the centre of the mandapam is a large platform with polished black stone pillars and a canopy fully covered with wood carvings of a very high order. The mandapam is reputed to have been

The majestic wide view that shows the colorful ceiling

built by Vyagrapathar Chokkanatha Nayakar whose crudely sculptured statue is on a pillar in front of the platform. The important festival relating to Meenakshi Sundareshwarar's marriage takes place here annually. A stone relief of Gundodhara is on one of the side walls and is reported to have been brought here from the Annakkuli Mandapam. A timbered hall has been erected in front of this mandapam by the Nattukkottai Chettiars in recent years. This hall with its timber roofing and beautifully wrought wooden beams is the only structure of its kind in the whole of the temple and is a good specimen of contemporary craftsmanship.

Gopurams

The lofty towers that have the art work of all aspects available in nature are a unique feature that characterizes an Indian temple. These towers were built to be viewed from a distance and it was an indication of a city or town nearby. The tower tells a story by itself. Most of the fables found in Hindu Mythology find a place on these towers. For example one can find the art work of The Divine Sport in detail on the towers of the Madurai Meenakshi Temple. The details and colors used on these towers speak of the artistic development of our culture much before the influence of foreign invaders. The tower that surmounts the Sanctum is generally called the *Vimana* while the ones on the outer walls and vestibules is the *Gopuram*.

Inside view of Raja Gopuram

Outer Gopurams

The four main outer *gopurams* on the east, west, north and south of the Madurai temple have a singular beauty and grace of their own. They have won the admiration of the visitors and the appreciation of the critics. Many temple *gopurams* come second only to this piece of construction in architectural proportion or artistic embellishments. The creators of the Madurai temple had a fine sense of artistry and the towering outer *gopurams* are standing monuments to their genius.

View from top to bottom of Raja Gopuram

The grand aerial view in which all the gopurams are visible that brought fame to the city of Madurai

Bangle Seller Episode

Lord Shiva once took the form of Bhikshatanar (Mendicant) and visited the hermitages of the Rishis of Darukavanam (Ascetics of the Daruka forest) for the ultimate purpose of ridding them of their arrogance. When Bhikshatanar went round seeking alms from the hermits, the wives of the Rishis were enchanted by the charming Bhikshatana which infuriated the Rishis. The wives were cursed to be reborn as women in the trading community in Madurai. When they pleaded release from the curse they were informed that when the Supreme Lord of Madurai comes into contact with their hands the curse will be lifted. Long afterwards, Somasundarar took the form of a bangle seller and while vending bangles in the streets of Madurai adorned the hands of these ladies of the Vanigar street with bangles and thus released them from the curse of the rishis. This episode which appears as the 32nd in Thiruvilayadal Puranam is reenacted on the seventh day of the Avani Moolam festival when the Lord will be decorated as the Bangle seller and worshipped.

The East Gopuram

Like the other *gopurams*, the base of the east *gopuram* is a stone structure of two storeys. The center has the projected portico. There is a marked similarity among all the *gopurams*. However, there are the slight details variations that make them stand apart as individual towers of excellence. The subtle changes in the ornamentation escape the casual observer.

The east *gopuram* is considered to be the oldest among the outer *gopurams* but very few vestiges of the earlier structure are in existence today. With 9 tiers, the height of *gopuram* is 153 feet and base measures 111 feet in length and 65 feet in width. It carries 1011 architectural stucco images. These are done with such detail that it needs a close look at them to understand the tell tale marks of the sculptors.

The door of the east *gopuram* of which only one leaf is in position today is a huge specimen (about 35 feet) running the whole height of the entrance and is a remarkable example of the wood carver's art.

The brick superstructure repeats the native materials motif in all its nine tiers. Much of the older stucco figures have been replaced by modern figures many of which relate to the Divine Sport legends. This *gopuram* with its well-marked vertical and horizontal divisions is an imposing tower.

Inside the entrance to the east *gopuram* called the *Kilaigopuram* are two inscriptions. The style and architectural design indicates that the building of the *gopuram* must have commenced during some earlier Pandiya King in the later part of the 12th Century. The finish and the art work on the upper tiers gives the impression that Jatavarman Sundara Pandyan I (1256 A.D.) was probably the final builder of this *gopuram* who must have given the finishing touches to this grand structure.

East Tower constructed by Jatavarman Sundara Pandyan I 1256 AD bears 1100 Mythological figures.

Stone inscription in East Gopuram

Stone inscription in East Gopuram

West Gopuram

Although the southern side *gopuram* finds more visitors to the temple, it is the West *gopuram* that has many features that tell a tale of the creator's period. The story that is told by the representation of stucco figures is a treasure that has to be cherished. It lies in West Adi veedi that also has many relics of an older structure mainly noticeable on the ground floor of its base. The whole surface of this structure is covered with stucco figures of legendary and iconographic nature. Notable among these are the stucco figure of the "Churning of the Ocean" and figures of Rishabharudar. This *gopuram* is 154 feet high with a base of 101 feet length and 63 feet width and is embellished with 1124 stucco images

This nine storeyed west *gopuram* was built by Parakrama Pandyan in about 1323 A.D. Inside the entrance of the *gopuram* are a Pandya fish crest and an inscription in verse form in praise of Parakarma Pandyan.

West Tower built by Parakrama Pandyan during his reign 1315 -1347 AD bears 1124 Mythological Figures.

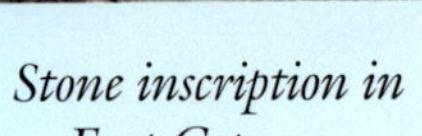

Stone inscription in East Gopuram

South Gopuram

Due to its picturesque situation near the Golden Lily Tank the south *gopuram* is the most photographed of all the *gopurams* of the Madurai temple. This *gopuram* is probably the most viewed part of the city and has become synonymous with the temple.

Structurally it is also one of the most beautiful. The two tiers of its high stone base are well proportioned and give an imposing appearance. The intervals between projecting bays and recesses are well spaced and architecturally the whole structure is in very good taste. The entire construction is perhaps of late 16th century with late Vijayanagar and early Madurai or Nayakar characteristics. All the wall pilasters of the south gopuram have the Vijayanagar type of squatting lions at their base.

The south *gopuram* at 160 feet height is the tallest of the outer *Gopurams*. Its base is 108 feet long and 67 feet wide and the entire tower is embellished with an astonishing 1511 stucco images.

The brick super structure is of singular beauty and the myriad stucco figures enhance its architectural construction. The sloping edges of the South *Gopuram* have concave sweeping curve that is more pronounced than the other three *gopurams* giving it a singular elegance. The *gopuram* was built by Siramalai Sewandhi Moorthy Chettiar.

Bottom: South Tower built by Siramalai Sevanthi Murthy Chetti bears 1511 Mythological Figures. One can clearly see the concave sweep along the sloping edges

The most photographed view that this South Gopuram offers is summed up in this photo from the steps of the Golden Lotus pond with the figurines in the foreground.

North Gopuram

This *gopuram* may not have the sheen or popularity that is enjoyed by the other *gopurams* but it still has its presence felt with its towering height. Till recent years the North *Gopuram* was an incomplete structure, though its base indicated that it was meant to be the same as the others with 9 tiers. Being without the stucco figures or roof it was called the *mottai gopuram*, that is, the bald-headed *gopuram*. It is still known as the *mottai gopuram* although it has now got a roof which was built by the Nattukkotai chettiyars about the end of the nientheth century. The stone base of the *gopuram* is in two storeys as on the other *gopurams*.

Overall the completed *Gopuram* is 152 feet in height with the base of 111 feet length and 66 feet width embellished with 404 stucco Images. Going inside one of the storeys of the north *gopuram* one learns much about the mode of construction of these *gopurams*. Stone pillars are used on the different floor levels and wooden beams and rafters are used to support the terraces.. The stone pillars at the front of the opening have a bulbous capital and a wooden corbel of the early lotus bud type. This *gopuram* has cubicles and a carved ceiling with stone decorations similar to those in the south *gopuram*.

Architecturally the north *gopuram* might be assigned to the 16th-17th Century. Literary evidences also support this date and indicate that Krishna Virappar Nayaker, (1564-72) the grandson of Viswanatha Nayakar and the builder of the Kambattadi Mandapam, constructed the north gopuram. Mottaikopuram is a structure without a tower.

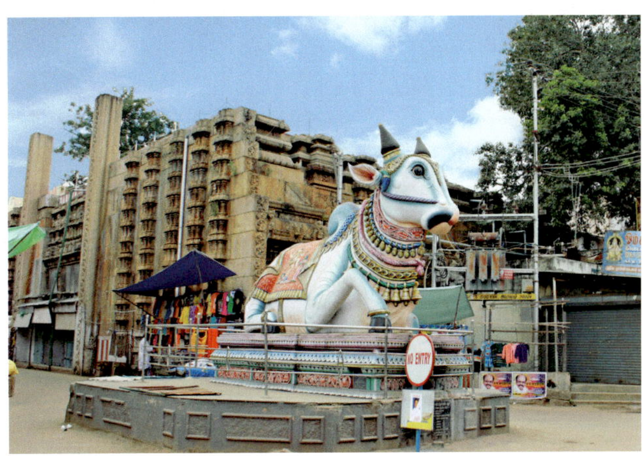

Raya Gopuram

The Raya *Gopuram* which is to the east of the Pudu Mandapam is nearly twice the size of the base of the east *gopuram* and measures 174 feet by 117 feet. The height of the first tier is 57 feet. It is a stupendous structure and if it had been completed it would have been one of the biggest *gopurams* in South India. The building owes its origin to Thirumalai Nayakar who is also reported to have built similar unfinished *gopurams* in numerous other centres in South India. The monolithic pillars of the Raya *Gopuram* are over 50 feet high and mark the high degree of proficiency which Dravidian stone masons had attained. The *gopuram* base is intricately finished and ornamented. Its pavilion pillars, its lion-based pilasters and the carvings display a keen sense of massive proportions and large-scale ornamentation. There are many reliefs of Thirumalai Nayakar and his queens and a figure of Meenakshi coronation on the wall surface. In its corbels and cornices this *gopuram* establishes the Madurai style of architecture which dates from about this time. It is a pity that this noble pile should be surrounded by sordid human habitations. A comparison with old photographs of the site taken nearly 100 years ago would show that the road level here has considerably risen so that much of the base of the *gopuram* is today below ground level.

Left: North Tower started by Krishnaveerappanaicker (1564-1572) and completed by the Amaravathi Pudur VayinagaramNagappa Chetti in 1878 CE.

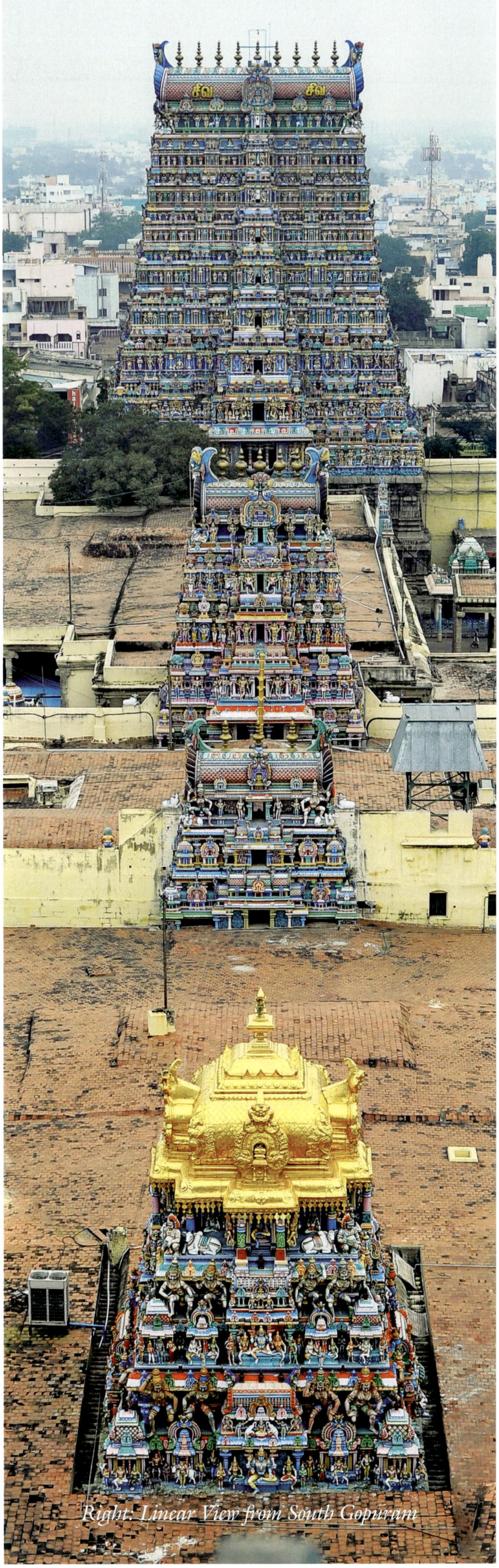

Right: Linear View from South Gopuram

Inner Gopurams

The inner *gopurams* rise up to the expectations of the visitor after the massive outer *gopurams*. There are eight in number of which only the Chitra *gopuram* is seven tiered.

The Chitra Gopuram

This is in line with the Amman Sannidhi *gopuram* which was perhaps the original entrance to the sanctum. This *gopuram* measures 117 feet high, 38 feet in length and 78 feet in width and is attributed to Kalatthi Mudali, son of Aryanatha Mudali, 1570 A.D. The architectural style also supports this date.

Gopura Nayaka Gopuram

The Gopura Nayaka *gopuram* which leads to the main Sanctum (Swami Sannidhi) is a five-storeyed one and an inscription to the right of the entrance credits Visvappar, the son of Iswarappar, during the reign of the Vijayanagara king Acyutar (1529-42 A.D.) for having built it for the king.

Nadu Kattu Gopuram

The Nadu Kattu *gopuram*, as its name indicates, is between the Amman and Swami shrines. It is a five storeyed structure and its style, like that of the Gopura Nayaka *gopuram*, is that of the mid-sixteenth century. The height of *gopuram* measures 69 feet with 33 feet base length and 44 feet width which carries 112 stucco figures.

Both *gopurams* are ornamented with many beautiful niche figures. The stone carving is of a high order. *Bhairavar* and *Virabadrar* are sculptured in the niches of the Gopura Nayaka *gopuram*, while *Natarajar* and *Shanmukhar* are in the niches of Nadu kattu *gopuram*. Construction of this *Gopuram* is attributed to Sira Malai Sevvandhi Murthi in the year 1559 AD.

Kadaka Gopuram

Architecturally the Kadaka *gopuram* which was the western entrance to the Amman Sannidhi could be the oldest among the *gopurams*. This was built by *Varathumbicchi* in the year 1570 A.D. and it has 5 tiers, with a height of 64 feet, basement of 50 feet length and 28 feet width which accommodates 280 stucco images.

Palakai Gopuram

This is next to the Kadaka *gopuram* and was the western entrance to the Swami shrine. The renovation was done by Mallappan in the year 1374 A.D. It is of 72 feet height with 5 tier, the basement being 40 feet length and 31 feet width showing 340 stucco images. The Palakai *gopuram* is the model for many of the modem *gopurams* constructed in the present day.

Chinna Mottai Gopuram

The five-storeyed Chinna Mottai *gopuram* is on the northern side of the Swami Sanctum *gopuram*. It is in many ways similar to the Gopura Nayaka and the Nadukattu *Gopuram*, being constructed about the same period, by Sevvandhi Velan in the year 1560 A.D.

Sannidhi Gopuram

The two Sannidhi *gopurams* are perhaps two of the earliest structures existing in the temple. Much of the architectural details of the Swami Sanctum *Gopuram* base remain hidden behind structures built later on and very little of it is visible. The early part of the structure may perhaps date about the 13th-14th centuries.

The base of the Amman Sannidhi *gopuram* has also early features. Parts of the two Sannidhi *gopurams* may perhaps belong to a period between the 12th-13th centuries, the Swami Sannidhi *gopuram* belonging to the 12th-l3th centuries while the Amman Sanctum may belong to the latter half of the 13th century.

All the inner *gopurams* are must - see structures that add value and aesthetics to the wonderful temple.

Breathtaking spectacular View from West Gopuram Tower of Madurai Temple Complex

View of the South Gopuram with 1511 stucco figures .

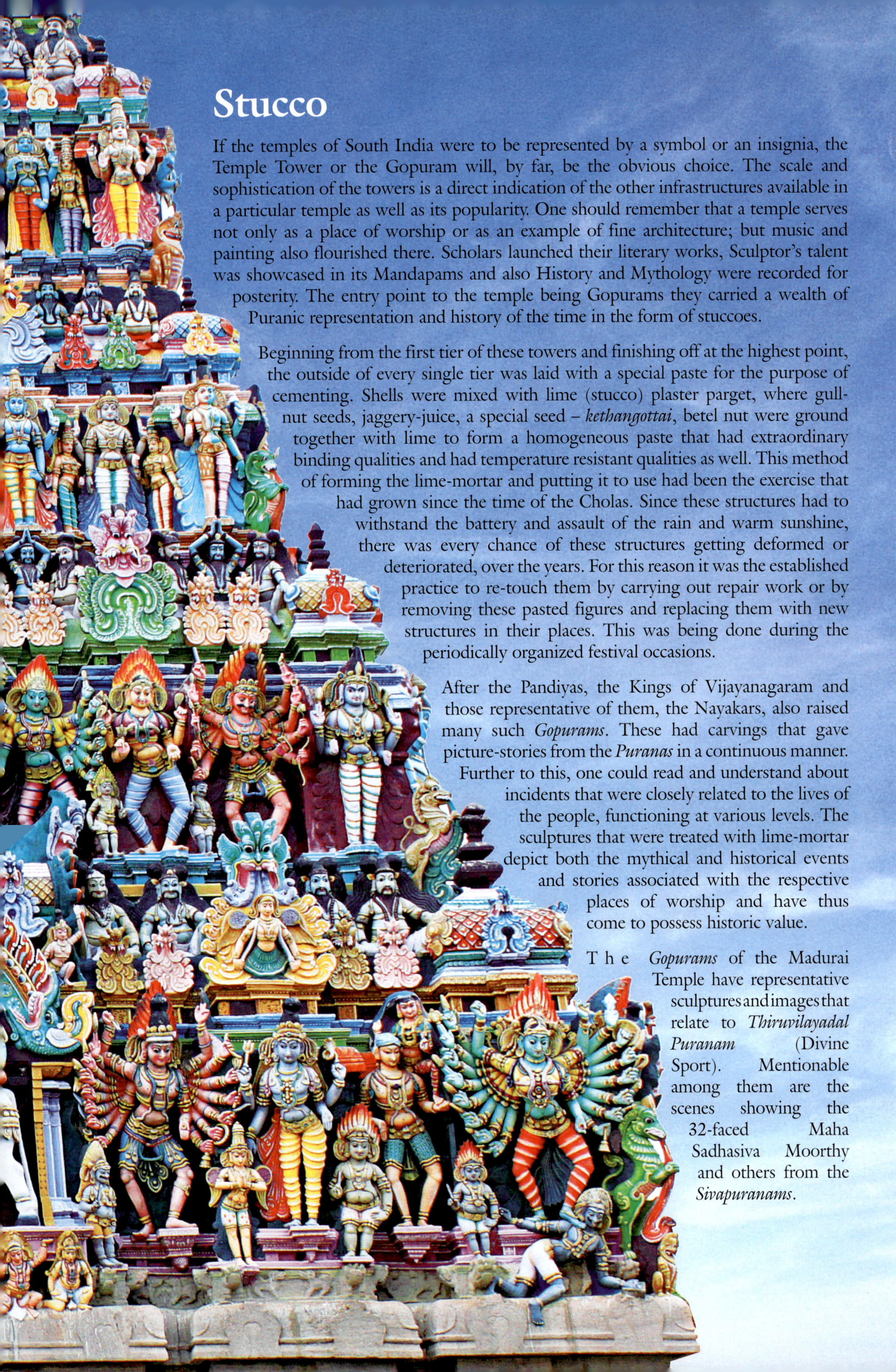

Stucco

If the temples of South India were to be represented by a symbol or an insignia, the Temple Tower or the Gopuram will, by far, be the obvious choice. The scale and sophistication of the towers is a direct indication of the other infrastructures available in a particular temple as well as its popularity. One should remember that a temple serves not only as a place of worship or as an example of fine architecture; but music and painting also flourished there. Scholars launched their literary works, Sculptor's talent was showcased in its Mandapams and also History and Mythology were recorded for posterity. The entry point to the temple being Gopurams they carried a wealth of Puranic representation and history of the time in the form of stuccoes.

Beginning from the first tier of these towers and finishing off at the highest point, the outside of every single tier was laid with a special paste for the purpose of cementing. Shells were mixed with lime (stucco) plaster parget, where gull-nut seeds, jaggery-juice, a special seed – *kethangottai*, betel nut were ground together with lime to form a homogeneous paste that had extraordinary binding qualities and had temperature resistant qualities as well. This method of forming the lime-mortar and putting it to use had been the exercise that had grown since the time of the Cholas. Since these structures had to withstand the battery and assault of the rain and warm sunshine, there was every chance of these structures getting deformed or deteriorated, over the years. For this reason it was the established practice to re-touch them by carrying out repair work or by removing these pasted figures and replacing them with new structures in their places. This was being done during the periodically organized festival occasions.

After the Pandiyas, the Kings of Vijayanagaram and those representative of them, the Nayakars, also raised many such *Gopurams*. These had carvings that gave picture-stories from the *Puranas* in a continuous manner. Further to this, one could read and understand about incidents that were closely related to the lives of the people, functioning at various levels. The sculptures that were treated with lime-mortar depict both the mythical and historical events and stories associated with the respective places of worship and have thus come to possess historic value.

T h e *Gopurams* of the Madurai Temple have representative sculptures and images that relate to *Thiruvilayadal Puranam* (Divine Sport). Mentionable among them are the scenes showing the 32-faced Maha Sadhasiva Moorthy and others from the *Sivapuranams*.

Festival Traditions

Man and society are inter-dependent. Temples provided an excellent platform for social networking. Special occasions were created that offered opportunities for people to meet to mingle in the temples.

The temple festivals are primarily religious in character and provide opportunity for people at large to get together and fulfill religious obligations and vows. The time of festivals synchronized with solstices, equinoxes, full moon, new moon and other astronomical phenomena, when people believed that the earth was influenced by celestial bodies and a dip in a sacred river or water-source would result in their physical, emotional and spiritual well-being.

Incidentally these festival occasions generated great commercial activity with the result that in course of time they assumed socio-economic roles. In view of this, the powers that be, the rulers, took deeper interest in them and enlarged the scope and form of these festivals.

After the period of the Pandyas from 1350 AD, to about 400 years later, when the Vijayanagara empire and the Nayak kings came to power, new initiatives were introduced in the architecture and festivals developed further in colour and form.

The temple started playing a greater role in the lives of people as festivities and rituals connecting the temple with the general public were brought into practice. Tirumalai Nayakar, the great Nayak King who ruled from Madurai, conceived the idea of the *"Chithirai Thiruvizha"* which takes place in the Tamil month of *Chithirai*. During this festival, the daily festivities in the Meenakshi temple culminate in the wedding of the Goddess to Lord Sundareshwarar. The deities of the nearby temples were also brought in and beautiful tales woven around them. An interesting story is that of Azhagar (Vishnu) who comes in the form of Lord Kallazhagar from the nearby Azhagar Koil to attend His sister's wedding but is disappointed that the Wedding is over. He becomes angry and turns back to go to his abode. The festivities are extended by two more days to appease Lord Kallazhagar till he returns to Azhagar Koil. The Nayak king had beautifully bridged Saivite and Vaishnavite tradition with this festival.

During the period of the Nayakars, the practice of constructing separate shrines for the Goddess also started. Halls with Hundred pillars, Thousand pillars and Marriage halls and Multipurpose halls were built around the temples. The pillars of such halls were sculpted beautifully with statues of Gods, humans and of *Yali*, the mythical lion.

The Pudu Mandapam (New Hall) at Madurai built at basement level near the temple served as a place for the various monthly rituals for the Goddess and for cultural performances. According to Rizwan Salim in his book "Need for cultural Pride – Revival", "Ancient Hindu Temple architecture is the most awe inspiring, ornate and spell binding architectural style found anywhere in the world. No artists of any historical civilization have ever revealed the same genius as ancient Hindu artists and artisans".

Annual Festivals of the Temple

Festivals are celebrated in this temple throughout the year. Some of the most popular festivals of the temple are *Chithirai* festival, *Avanimoola* festival, *Masi* Mandala festival, Float festival, and *Navarathri* cultural festival.

Month of April (Chithirai)

The *Chithirai* festival is celebrated for 12 days during the Tamil month of *Chithirai* (April in the English calendar) and begins with the flag hoisting on the first day. On the 8th day the coronation of Meenakshi Amman takes place. On the 9th day the Goddess is taken out in procession. On the 10th day the celestial wedding of Goddess Meenakshi and Lord Sundareshwarar is performed, followed by car festival the next day. *Theertha* festival (Holy Bathing Festival) is celebrated on the 12th day with the Lord and Goddess going around the Masi streets.

Month of May (Vaikasi)

The spring festival is hosted for ten days during this month. On the 10th day milk and mango would be offered to the deities. The Lord and Goddess would proceed to the Pudhu Mandapam, and be taken out in procession from there. On the day of *Moola* star, the procession of 63 Saints would be conducted in the morning and at night Thirugnanasambandar would be taken out in procession.

Month of June (Aani)

Oonjal festival is conducted for ten days during this month. On the 10th day, the triple fruit pooja would be performed. *Abhishekam* for Sivakami Amman and Arulmighu Natarajar would be performed on the day of *Uthiram*. The Panchasabha Nataraja Moorthy would be taken out in procession along the four Masi streets.

Month of July (Aadi)

The Aadi *Mulaikottu* festival is celebrated for 10 days during this month. The festival is confined only to the Amman, who will be taken out in procession along the Aadi streets. Special recitals of *Nadaswaram* are usually the highlight of this festival.

Month of August (Aavani)

The *Aavani* festival is conducted for 18 days. Six days of the festival would be devoted to Arulmighu Chandrasekarar and the balance 12 days would be for the *Panchamoorthies*. On the 7th day of the festival, coronation would be performed for Sundareshwarar and on the 8th day the horse reins would be exchanged. On the 9th day the episode of Lord Shiva carrying soil for earning *pittu* would be enacted while the holy water festival on the occasion of the joining of *Avittam* and *Pooranai* would be celebrated. On the same night, Arulmighu Thirupparankundram Subramaniyar and Thiruvadhavur Arulmighu Manickavasaka would bid farewell. During the festival of Chandrasekarar,

The first respects duly bestowed on the temple trustee at the beginning of the festivities

procession would be taken out along the second corridor of Swami Shrine. The *Panchamoorthies* would be taken around in procession along Aavani Moola streets. During these days the ten miracles performed by the Lord of Madurai would be enacted by the *Sivachariars*.

Month of September (Purattasi)

The *Navarathri* festival is celebrated for Amman in a grand manner during this month. Goddess Meenakshi would appear in resplendent dress and bless the devotees at the `kolu mandapam' in Amman Shrine. *Kalpa pooja* and *Laksharchana* would be performed everyday for the Amman at the sanctum. On the 10th day the washing of hair ceremony would be performed. On that *Panchamoorthies* would be taken out in procession within the temple premises. On all ten days of the festival, cultural events would be hosted in a grand manner. The entire temple complex would be bathed in color lamps and the dolls would be arranged in a manner befitting the festive occasion.

The Goddess being taken around on the Golden Horse.

Wedding of Meenakshi with Sundareshwarar

On the tenth day of the chithirai Festival the Wedding of Meenakshi with Sundareshwarar is celebrated. This takes place at the junction of the west Aadi veedhi and the north Aadi veedhi near Thiruppugazh Mandapam. In this festival both Lord Subrahmanya and Pavalakkanivay Perumal also participate. One Shiva priest takes the role of Sundareswarar and other the role of Meenakshi and exchange garlands. Thirumangalyam is presented to Menakshi and traditional ceremonies as in any Hindu marriage are also performed. The accompanying picture shows the grand wedding scene of the Divine Couple.

The decorated idols of the Lord and Goddess during the celestial wedding. Millions of devotees gather to get a view of this grand form. The couple decked in finest dresses and jewelry is taken around on the chariot

Goddess Meenakshi on the Parrot Vahanam

Month of October (Aipasi)

Kolattam festival is conducted for six days during this month. For five days Amman would be taken out in procession along the Aadi streets while on the sixth day both *Amman* and *Swamy* would be taken out in procession. Women would dance *kolatttam* (striking short sticks together). It is during this month, that *Pavithrotsavam* would take place. Chandrasekarar would be taken in procession along the second corridor of Lord's Shrine.

Kanda Sashti fesival would be celebrated for six days at the Koodal Kumarar Sannidhi. Unlike in Thiruchandur, *Soorasamharam* is not performed here. On the seventh day when Arulmighu Muthukumarar goes out in procession, `*Pavadai Dharshan'* would be conducted.

On the day of Deepavali festival, a king's court would be held for the employees of the temple. On the days of *Pooram* in this month, the ceremony of hoisting and swinging Meenakshi Amman would be performed.

Month of November (Karthigai)

Deepam (lights) festival would be conducted for ten days during this month. *Swamy* would be taken out in procession along the Aadi streets. On the day of *Karthigai* one lakh lamps would be lit in the temple. On that day a bonfire would be lit in East Masi street.

Glowing oil lamps adorn the Golden Lotus Pond and its steps during Karthigai Deepam festival. The lights and the glow give an impression of a celestial ambience on that occasion.

Lord Sundareswara on
Kailasa Paravatham Vahanam

Goddess Meenakshi decorated with crown made of pearls

Month of December (Margazhi)

Oil anointing ceremony is conducted for nine days in this month at the New Mandapam. Arulmigu Meenakshi Amman would be taken out in procession along the Chitrai streets. On the day of *Thiruvadhirai, Arudhra Dharshan* will take place. *Pancha Sabha* Nataraja *Murthigal* would be taken in procession along the Masi streets. On the day of *Ashtami* the Lord and Goddess would ride the oxen vehicle and go round Kottai streets. *Thiruvembavai* festival would be conducted for ten days. Everyday, Arulmighu Manickavasagar would be taken out in procession along Aadi streets in the mornings. On the 10th day rotating wheel and golden spring ceremonies would be conducted. In the mornings *Thiruvembavai* and *Thirupalli Yezhutchi* lyrics would be recited with religious discourses by spiritual leaders. Competitions would be conducted for school and college students and prizes distributed.

Month of January (Thai)

The float festival is conducted for 12 days during the month. *Swamy* and *Amman* would be taken out in procession along the Chitra streets. On the 8th day the casting of net festival would be held while *theertham* festival and the pushing of the float would be held on the 10th day. On the 11th day harvesting of sheaves and on the 12th day the float festival would be conducted.

The celestial wedding being replayed for which millions throng the temple for this once a year event from all over the world. This event made the city of Madurai world famous.

Presenting Gold Staff to Dharumi

The Pandya king once was taking a walk in his garden with the queen when he perceived a sweet scent emanating from the tresses of his queen. He wanted to know whether this is natural or artificial for which purpose he announced a competition among the poets of his court. Whoever composes a convincing poem on the issue would be rewarded with a purse of 1000 gold coins. He caused a staff filled with thousand gold coins to be hung at the gate of the Sangam hall to be claimed by the winner. Now, Dharumi was a poor devotee of Somasundarar belonging to *Adhi Saiva* group who was daily praying to the Lord seeking funds for his wedding ceremony. Somasundarar took pity on the devotee's plight and wrote a verse on the subject of the king's doubt, gave it to Dharumi and sent him to claim the gold staff from the king. While all the poets in the Sangam assembly appreciated the verse and had no hesitation in according the prize to him, Nakkeerar objected to it claiming that the verse was faulty in content. Dharumi went back to the Lord and narrated the whole event, on which Somasundarar himself took the form of a poet and debated with Nakkeerar to win the argument and hand over the gold coins to Dharumi. This episode is reenacted on the fourth day of the Avani Moolam festival even to this day. Fifty Second episode in Thiruvilayadal Puranam describes this divine sport.

Month of February (Maasi)

The Maasi Mandala festival is conducted for a *mandalam* (48 days). Six days of the festival is devoted to Arulmighu Vinayaka, six days for Arulmighu Kumar, three days for the trinity and six days for Chandrasekarar. The deities would be taken out in procession along the second corridor of Swamy Sannidhi. Panchamoorthy festival would be celebrated for ten days, when they are taken out in procession along the Chitra streets. *Theertham* would be held on the day of *Maham*. Silent festival would be conducted for nine days of which three days would be for Chandrasekarar and an equal number of days for Swamy and Chandikeswarar. On the 10th day, the flag would be lowered and accounts read.

Month of March (Panguni)

The summer spring festival is hosted for nine days at the Velliaymbala mandapam. Swamy and Amman would be taken in procession along *Chitra* streets. On the day of *Panguni Uthiram*, *Swamy* and Amman would proceed to Arulmighu Thiruvappudayar temple and bless those who excel in their religious belief by sprinkling `rasa vadham'.

The illuminated temple on the occasion of the float festival

The Golden Nandi, which is the vehicle of the Lord Sundareshwarar which is a unique feature of this temple on which the Lord and Goddess are seated.

Liberation to a Stork

There was a Stork living on the banks of a tank feeding on fish and other marine life. Once the stork saw in a pond ascetics taking bath and several fish sliding on their bodies as they performed their ablutions.The Stork did not want to feed on those fish which had physical contact with the holy bodies of the ascetis. It also learnt from the conversations of the ascetics about the holy city of Madurai and its presiding deity Somasundarar. The stork, propelled by a burning desire to visit Madurai went to the Golden Lotus pond and took residence there. Though tempted to feed on the fish at the Lotus pond, the stork restrained itself considering it a sin to kill for food at such a holy place. It also beseeched the Lord to grant salvation, not only to itself but also to all its clan. The Lord took compassion on the Stork and not only granted salvation to the stork but also ordained that there will be no marine life in the Lotus pond so that all avian visitors to the pond will not have to feed there. This episode of salvation to Stork is celebrated in the second day of the Avani Moolam Festival and the Lord is appropriately decorated.

The Chariot Festival

The Chariot Festival is indeed a marvellous event where men and women from all strata of society gleefully participate. This festival is a unique one, as here is a case where the Lord not only showers mercy on those who worship him, but makes a journey, seeks his disciples and blesses them. The chariot itself is an attractive piece, placed on a pedestal, something quite similar to that in which the main deity is seated inside the temple, with a special rostrum, and a special structure over it. Representations showing the historic significance of the place of worship have been carved on wood on this chariot - a beguiling presentation by itself.

This festival would happen on the day following Meenakshi-Sundareshwarar's grand marriage function in Madurai. There would be two separate chariots, one for Meenakshiammai and the other for Sundareshwarar and these two deities would go around separately. The immortal work *"Thiruppani Maalai"* reveals to us that this *Ther* (Chariot) Festival was in vogue even before the reign of Thirumalai Naicker. The fact that the Chariot went around Masi Streets (*Veedhi*) is perhaps an indication that this festival was held in the Tamil month of Masi. The chariots of today have been formed and offered by VijayaRanga Chokkanadha Nayakar, the grandson of Rani Mangammal. Details of The Divine Sport of Lord Shiva (*Thiruvilayadal Puranam*) and of *Sivakami Puranam* are sculpted on the chariot that belonged to Sundareshwarar.

Lord as the Firewood Seller

Once a Yazh exponent (a stringed instrument similar to veena) from north India by name Emanathan paid a visit to the Royal Cort at Madurai. He won great acclaim at the court and a lot of presents for his musical talent from the king. He became puffed up with pride since Madurai had no one to challenge him. The king, in a dejected mood, arranged for Banabathiran, the court musician to offer competition to Emanathan. Banabathiran being a devout worshipper of Somasundarar, beseeched the Lord to save him as he knew his musical talents had no chance against a formidable adversary like Emanathan. The Lord took pity on his devotee and took the form of a firewood seller and reached the guest house where Emanathan was staying. Parking himself on the piol of the guest house he sang a short piece in tune with his Yazh. Struck by the supreme melody and sweetness of the music, Emanathan wanted to know who the firewood seller was. The other replied he was a drop out from the school of Banabathiran. Emanathan hastily packed his bags and scooted thinking to himself that if a drop out can sing so well the master would surely be out of this world and the best way to save his skin was to disappear from the scene. The king and Banabathiran came to know of what happened next day and praised the Lord profusely. This episode is celebrated on the tenth day of Avani Moolam Festival when the Lord is decked up as a firewood seller.

Temple Car

All big temples would usually possess a temple chariot (car) on which the Lord or Goddess would be taken out in procession. The bigger the chariot is, the more prosperous the temple and prouder are its citizens. The celestial chariot, depending on its size would have two to nine wheels to move it around. Sundareshwarar's Chariot is the pride of the temple and people of the city.

The first row carries the images of goblins and the second layer carries those of Gods/Goddesses and the mythological animal (*Yali*). It is in the third portion that one will be able to see figures of dimension 1 x 1.5 feet that depict the sculptures of Lord Shiva's *Puranas* and saintly images. The second portion and in its first and second rows one can find miniature structures and *Yalis* exhibiting fine and astute craftsmanship.

In the Second portion, particularly in the third row of this Chariot, one can get to see scenes from the *Thiruvilayadal Puranam* (Divine Sport). The third, fourth and fifth portions show the customary dance and the distinctive stick-dance as well. It is reasonable to think that these dances would have been performed in front of the Chariot as it embarked on its journey.

The grand celestial chariot with its fantastic craftsmanship seen in its carvings.

Coronation of Meenakshi Amman

Madurai city is often called the 'City of Festivals'. Major Festivals of Meenakshi temple are the Float Festival, the Chithirai Festival, and the Avani Moolam Festival. These are primarily meant for public benefit and go by the name 'Sambhavi Deekshai'. The Festivals particularly benefit those who are unable to go to the temple and worship the Lord; the Lord himself deciding to come around the streets in procession.

Chithirai Festival is one such famous festival, which takes place for twelve days. On the eighth day Coronation of Meenakshi Amman is celebrated. On that occasion, the chief trustee of the temple takes the role of the Pandya King and presents the Sceptre to Goddess Meenakshi in a very impressive ceremony. The sight of Goddess Meenakshi in her coronation dress is a never-to-miss spectacle.

Coronation of the Goddess that shows her decorated with all the finest jewelry.

Ornaments

One cannot see such a large collection of ornaments of gold, silver and precious stones all together except at this Meenakshi Temple here in Madurai. The jewels adorned by the Goddess speak volumes of her devotees' offering to the temple.

The Meenakshi temple is central to life and culture of the people of Madurai. The successive kings that ruled over the Pandya Kingdom with Madurai as their capital city, held Goddess Meenakshi and Lord Sundareshwarar as the presiding deities of the Royal family. They believed that the fortunes of the city and the kingdom were dictated by the presiding deities. They vied with each other in offering expensive and rare jewellery with exquisite workmanship to both Meenakshi and Sundareshwarar. This practice was followed by other devotees as well, who took pleasure and pride in beautifying the image of Meenakshi and Sundareshwarar with jewellery suited for specific occasions or festivals.

For centuries Pandya kingdom was known for its pearls from Korkai and Thondi ports, which were exported to even far off places like Rome. It is but natural that both the deities have numerous ornaments, made out of pearls, intricately crafted with small and big pearls. Some of these are worth mentioning: *Muthu Chorukku, Muthu Uchikkondai, Muthu Mambazhakkondai*, (all used in hair do's), *Muthangi* (vest of pearls) *Muthumalai* (pearl necklaces), *Muthukkadivalam* (pearl rein) *Muthu Merkatte* are all used to adorn the deity during Navarathri festival.

History tells us that there was commerce in ancient times between Greece and Rome in the west and Tamil Nadu in the east. As if to signify this fact, there is a necklace of coins (*Kaasumalai*) from Rome available in the temple, presumably offered by the Romans to the deity of Madurai. Forty eight gold coins bearing Roman lettering are strung together in a silk thread interspersed with 50 golden drops. East India Company which occupied Madurai in 1790 has also donated a necklace of gold coins.

When Meenakshi appears riding a horse, she wears a head gear (*Thalaipahai Kireetam*) embossed with jewels donated by Thirumalai Nayakar.

An Englishman by the name Rous Peter was the Collector of Madurai in 1812 and an interesting anecdote is in circulation relating to his association with the temple. It is said that he used to go for a walk regularly around the temple and one day when it was raining heavily with lightning and thunder, he was sleeping in the upper floor of his residence. A girl suddenly appeared at his cot, and woke him up and ran down. The Collector followed the girl to the street and no sooner he was out of the house lightning struck the building which came crashing down. The Collector looked for the little girl presumably to thank her, only to see her enter the temple gate and disappear. In gratitude, the Collector decided to offer worship to Goddess Meenakshi in his own way and donated a pair of stirrups for the deity to be used when she appears on horseback in the temple festival. Each of these stirrups is encrusted with 211 rubies, 36 emeralds, 40 uncut diamonds, two pearls, two sapphires, and two cat's eyes. Even to-day whenever the Goddess comes out in procession on a horse, these stirrups are fitted.

Golden stirrups worn by the Goddess during the festival while going around the temple on horseback.

Nayakar has also donated other types of crowns to Goddess Meenakshi, a pearl crown interspersed with emeralds and diamonds and a head gear called *Thirimudi Chathu* (a head cover that sits on a lady's hair combed back and braided).

During the *Pattabhishekam* at *Avani Moolam* festival; the deity is adorned with a special crown of diamonds. Diamond stones are stacked together in a row and pure gold is inserted bit by bit in the interspaces and packed together firmly in this ornament. This type of unique setting goes by the name '*Kuudanakkattidam*' (cuudana structure) craftsmanship.

On the same occasion, the image of Sundareshwarar, carries a diamond scepter (*Rathina Sengol*) donated by Thirumalai Nayakar. During the *Kalyana Uttsavam* (divine wedding), a '*vasumalai*' crown is placed on the deity of Sundareshwarar. This crown shines with rare beauty and luster even though it is made up of unpolished rubies. One can enjoy on the *Avani Moolam* festival the sight of Lord Sundareshwarar decked up as a daily labourer, carrying a spade and basket ready to do the bidding of an old lady devotee for a handful of *pittu* (sweetened rice flour).

Bavani Sankar Sethupathy, the prince of Sivaganga has donated an ornament called '*Pottukkarai*', a necklace of gold embedded with emeralds and rubies. This chain is crafted with very fine gold wire, strong at the same time flexible, robust at the same time extremely smooth, so that it sits on the wearer's neck effortlessly. Another prince from the same lineage, Bhaskara Sethupathy of Ramanadapuram has donated a large finely crafted pendant.

There is also a noteworthy coral pendant constructed out of small branches of mature coral reef along with a coral *Thazhvadam* (long necklace). During the festival times devotees worship the images of the deity on different *vahanams* (vehicles) in the shape of *Nandi Devar* (the Divine Bull), *Karpaga Maram* (Divine Wish Fullfilling Tree), Horse, Elephant, *Bootham* (Divine Attendant) and *Yali* (Mythical Animal) and at that time ornament the deity with appropriate *vahana padakkangal* (Vehicle Medallions).

Vijayaranga Chokkanada Nayakar who ruled over Madurai, presented a golden chalice, known as '*chandana kumba*' for preparing sandal paste. It carries Telugu inscriptions. The images of Chandrasekar and Parvati in gold, an offering from Thirumalai Nayakar are placed on a swing every Friday evening for '*oonjal*' (swing) worship. Then there is a golden belt called '*Nagar Oddiyanam*' (snake shapped belt)

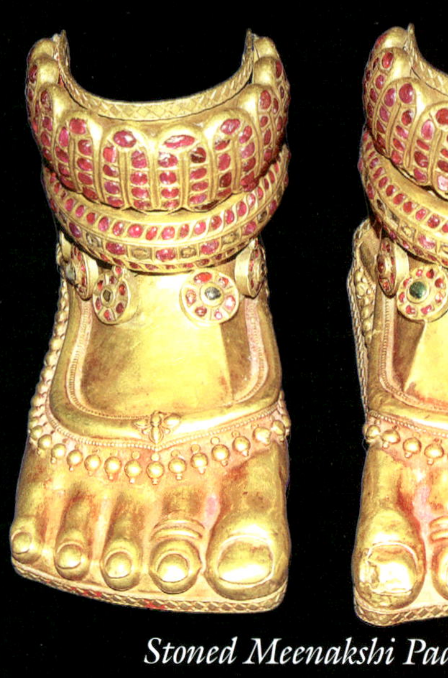

Stoned Meenakshi Paadam

Yali Face Thoda

Kreetam   *Crown*

Thilaka Kreetam

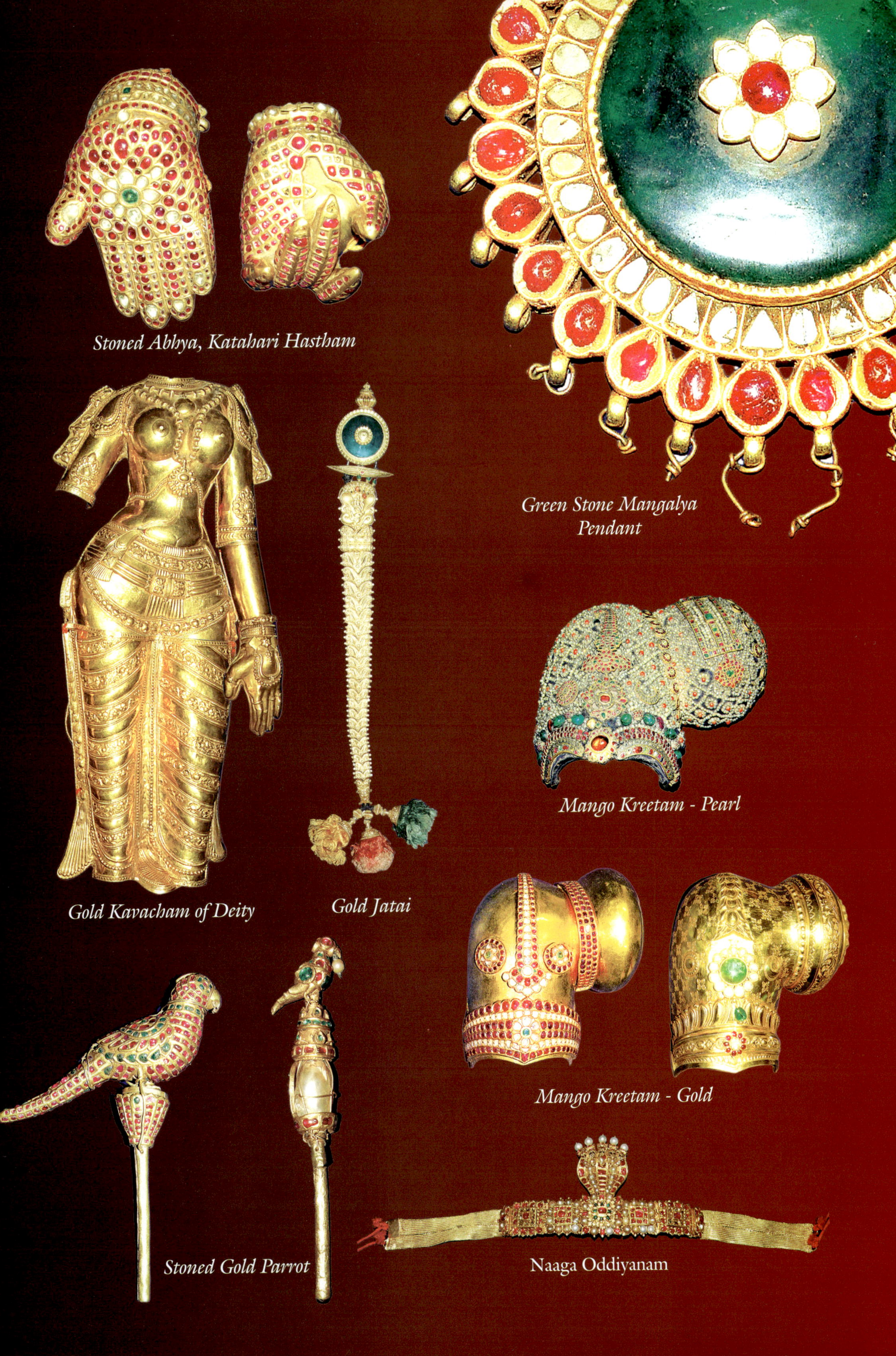

Stoned Abhya, Katahari Hastham

Green Stone Mangalya
Pendant

Gold Kavacham of Deity

Gold Jatai

Mango Kreetam - Pearl

Mango Kreetam - Gold

Stoned Gold Parrot

Naaga Oddiyanam

woven from gold strips with adjustable length and a head shaped like snake's hood. There is yet another pendant donated by Thirumalai Nayakar, beautifully embedded with large blue sapphire gems and shining with unmatched brilliance from which ever direction you look at it. This goes by the name *Neela Nayakka Padakkam* (Blue Nayakar Pendant). When Prince Edward VII visited India, he was wonder struck at the beauty of this pendant and carried it to London to show it to his mother Queen Victoria. It went all the way and back, and so earned the epithet 'London Returned Gem'.

There was a proprietor of a steamship, who had named his steam vessel SSM Meenakshi. He made a prayer that Goddess Meenakshi may protect his ship from any calamity in the high seas. Since his prayers were answered, he donated a huge silver vessel to the deity. Similarly many other devotees have also donated various articles of worship as well as ornaments; notable among them are two golden pots and a necklace of gold coins from Chettinad Nagarathars. Devotees often, as a part of their worship, arrange to adorn the deity with diamond crown, golden vest, etc. and arrange for a procession of the deity for all to see and appreciate.

Ornaments of Lord Sundareshwarar

Diamond Fore Head Ornament

Diamond Forhead ornament with Vilvaleaf

Chadamakuda Kuvalai (Sivlingam)

Golden Milk Vessel

Kalyana Kreeta

Summadu Kreeta

Thirumudi Kreeta

Pearl Thilaka Kreeta
Pearl Jata Makuta Kreeta
Coral Pendant
Ulava Kottai
Gold plated Chank
Mugal Kreeta
Ezhuthaani
Rayar Kreeta
Thilaka Kreeta
Neela Nayakka Padakkam

Bhikshatanar - the Lord as a beggar of Ego

The sages of Dharukavana, though they were doing penance, became arrogant and egocentric and started deviating from Bakthi marga, the path of wisdom. Lord Shiva decides to make them learn a lesson. So he transforms himself as a Bhikshatana, a beggar of alms. He takes along with him the lord Vishnu to Dharukavana, who is also transformed as a Mohini, an attractive woman. On seeing the gorgeous Mohini, the sages were enamored and fall head on heel in love with her. At the same time their wives too got attracted to the good-looking Bidshadana. They forget their penance entirely. Thus Lord Shiva teaches the sages the lesson by eliminating their ego. In Bidkshadana manifestation the lord Shiva seeks man instead of man seeking god and The Lord begs a total surrender of our egos, our self centered thoughts and our self consciousness completely. He also seeks love and compassion of our hearts.

The Azhagar Festival

Lord Vishnu's sister Parvathi was given in marriage to Shiva and in that manner becomes Shiva's brother-in-law. The *Puranas* give us this information. The Azhagar Festival is held to portray the significance of Sunderaraja Peruaman's formal visit to conduct the marriage of Meenakshi (who is but the manifestation of Perumal's sister Parvathi). He arrives at Madurai from Azhagar Kovil with all the attendant paraphernalia specifically brought from the bride's residence at the time of marriage. As he reaches the northern portion of the river *Vaigai*, he gets to know that the marriage has been solemnized. He therefore avoids the southern portion and goes back from the northern side. This has been the familiar story attached with this festival.

Kallazahagar after making his presence felt in *Vaigai* reaches Madurai, goes to Vandiyur and then reaches Thenur Mandapam the next day, where he grants deliverance from a damnable curse to Mandooga Maharishi. Then Kallazhagar proceeds to Karuppasamy temple and reaches Azhagar Kovil. At the auspicious time when Kallazhagar rises from the river *Vaigai*, Pavalakkanivaai Perumal, who is present in the Murugan Temple of Thirupparankundram, gets to the spot to welcome him.

Today, the marriage ceremony of Meenakshi-Sundareshwarar, the chariot festival closely associated with it and the rising of Kallazhagar from Vaigai, combine together to form the "Chithirai Thiruvizha" that is being celebrated with a sense of joy here, till this day. The Chariot festival is usually held on the next day after the holy marriage.

A sea of humanity at the site believed to be the place where Lord Vishnu entered the flooded river.

Lord Vishnu , while bringing gifts for his sister during her wedding faces a flooding river and manages to cross the rising river on horse back.

Pooja & Sevas

Amongst the Hindu Pantheon, even though the three primary responsibilities are assigned to the Creator – Brahma, the Preserver – Vishnu and the Destoryer – Shiva, the supreme deities are Shiva and Vishnu. Of the two, Vishnu is said to be Alankara Priya, one who loves being dressed up with various embellishments and jewels while Shiva is Abhisekapriya – one who is pleased with ablutions. Hence the rituals in the Meenakshi temple lay a lot of importance on the *Pujas* for Shiva and his consort Meenakshi.

The temple *pujas* fall under three categories, namely, *nitya pujas* which are done daily, *masaabishekam* which are performed once a month and thirdly *visesham* or festivals which are celebrated once a year.

Daily *pujas* are offered according to the *agama shastras* and are practically the same as they are in many Saiva temples. The ritual today is practically what it has been for hundreds of years. The *pujas* seem to have been performed six times in the day starting from the *Thiruvanandal pooja* in the early morning to the *Palliarai pooja* at night. The *nitya puja* at the two main shrines comprised the *abhishekam, dipa-aradhanai* and *naivedyam*. The *abhisheka dravyam* articles included are honey, tender coconuts, two sorts of sandal, plantain fruits, *paccakarpurm*, civet, sugar, curds, *parimaladravyam* or scents, benzoin, and *vibhuti*. The following were used for preparing the *naivedyams*: black gram and green gram, jaggery, tamarind, salt, pepper, cummin seeds, mustard and dil seeds, dry ginger, cardamom and rice. The *naivedyams* include eatable items made out of rice batter, pulses and cereals. During the day the Nityotsavar, Pallakku Sokkar, was taken on a procession three times a day round the *prakarams* of the temple with music and all honours. These *pujas* and customs are still observed in the present day.

The day begins with the rendering of the famous Thevaram in praise of Lord Shiva during which saivite scholar go around the temple singing the hymns.

Devotees vying with each other to pray to the holy fire in the belief that this would bring all prosperity and happiness in their lives.

The day's pujas conclude with offering of the holy water at the lotus feet of the Lord. After a full day's worship from devotees the Lord prepares to retire to the rest chamber.

The temple elephant which is housed inside the temple is taken around the premises while the morning prayers are offered.

Daily Pooja Schedules

Pooja Name	Days	Time
Thiruvanandal Pooja	Morning	05 : 00 AM - 06 : 00 AM
Vizha Pooja	Morning	06:30 AM - 07 : 15 AM
Kalasandhi Pooja	Morning	06:30 AM - 07 : 15 AM
Thrikalasandhi Pooja	Morning	10:30 AM - 11:15 AM
Uchikkala Pooja (Noon Pooja)	Morning	10:30 AM - 11:15 AM
Maalai Pooja	Evening	04:30 PM - 05:15 PM
Ardhajama Pooja (Night Pooja)	Night	07 : 30 PM - 08 : 15 PM
Palliarai Pooja	Night	09 : 30 PM - 10 : 00 PM

Worship Hours 5.00 am to 12.30 pm & 4.00 pm to 10.00 pm

For information please contact

Joint Commissioner / Executive Officer,
Arulmighu Meenakshi Sundareswarar Temple,
Madurai 625 001.
Telephone 091- 452- 2344360.
Fax 091- 452- 2341777
Email mmtemplejc@gmail.com

www.maduraimeenakshi.org

A

Aalavai Annal - Presiding deity of Madurai

Aavani Moolam - The day pertaining to moolam star in the tamil month of Avani(aug/sep)

Abhaya - A pose signifying protection

Adhisthanam – Establishment

Adhi Theertham - Name of a sacred tank

Agamas - Canonical text on temple- images & worship

Ambalam – Court

Ananda Tandava - Dance of Happiness

Antharalam - Passage connecting the shrine to the hall

Apasmara Purusha - Personification of ignorance

Arangetram - Inauguration

Ardha mandapam - Pillared hall in front of the shrine

Arukal pitham - Six pillared Hall

Asuras – Demons

Ashtasaktis - Eight powers

Ashtagajas - Eight elephants

Asthram - Weapon

Ashta Diggajangal - Eight elephants guarding the eight directions

Avani - A tamil Month

B

Brahmanams -Hindu sacred book

C

Chandra - Moon

Chakra peetam - Round base

Chinmudra - Posture of imparting wisdom

Chithirai - First tamil Month of the year.

Chithan - Realised soul

D

Damaru - Small drum

Dvarapalakas – Doorkeepers

G

Garbhagriha - Sanctum

Gada - A weapon of Vishnu

Gajasura -Elephant demon

Gajaari - Slayer of elephant-demon

Gnana – Knowledge

Gnanashakthi - Power of Knowledge

Gangaalam - Large vessel

Gopuram - Tower at the entrance or the gateway to a temple

H

Halasya Mahatmyam - History of Madurai in Sanskrit

I

Indira-Chief of Gods

Indravimanam - Vehicle of Lord Indra

Ichashakthi - Power of desire

J

Jalandharar - Shiva

Jatamakutam -Crown in the shape of bundled up hair

K

Kaala - Time / God of death

Kaasumalai - Chain made of coins

Kadambavana - Forest of kadamba trees; Madurai

Kamandalam -Water pot

Kandar Kali Venba - A hymn in praise of Lord Subramanya by Shri kumaragurupara

Kannikadanam - Giving away a bride in marriage

Kayal - Fish

Kapalam - Skull

Karandamakutam - A type of crown

Kilikkundu - The parrot cage

Kireetam - Crown

Kondai – Chignon

Kolu - Arrangement of idols

Kriyashakthi - Power to perform

kshethram - Holy place

Kumbapancarams - A pilaster with a pot base

Kumudam -Flower

Kurma - Tortoise

Kusa - Grass

L

Lakshacharna -Worship with a lakh names

Lilas - Sport

M

Maadakkoils - Raised temple

Maarukaal Thandavam - Cosmic dance of Siva with right leg lifted

Madhu – Honey

Mahanmiyam - Book extolling a place

Maha mandapam - The great assembly hall

Mambazhakkondai- Mango shaped chignon

Mandapam - Hall or pillared pavilion

Marga - Path

Mudhras -Postures

Mukhamandapam- The front portion in a Temple

Mrithunjaya -Shiva

N

Naan Maadak Koodal - Madurai

Nagarathars -People belonging to a particular place in Tamil Nadu

Nagasthiram-Serpent missile

Nandidevar -Shiva's bull

Naivedyams –Offerings

Navarathri -Nine day festival for Goddess

Nitya pujas- Daily Pooja

P

Padhigam - Sacred hymn

Padmasana -Lotus pose

Palliyarai - Divine bed chamber

Pancha Krithyas -Five activities

Panchaloha -Five metals

Pasupatastra -Name of a missile

Pavithrotsavam -Festival of purification

Parimaladravyam -Items that add aroma

Perumpanatruppadai - A tamil literary work

Pillaithamizh - A form of tamil poetry

Pitham -Base

Potramarai Kulam - Golden Lotus Tank

Prakarams - Parambulatory walk way around the sanctum

Pralaya -Deluge

Purusha –Human

Puthra Kameshti Yagam - A sacrifice for obtaining progeny

Purohit - Priest

S

Sabai or Sabha - Assembly/court/meeting hall

Sakthi - Power

Saptha – Seven

Sangam - Association of scholars

Saivism - School of Shiva worship

Shiva Lingams - An iconic form of Siva

Sikharam - Tower

Silapathikaram - One of the five great tamil poetic works during sangam period

Simhanandana - Tala rhythm in carnatic music

Siddhar - Ascetic

Siddhar - Ascetic

Soorasamharam- Slaying of demon Soora

Sthala Vruksham - Sacred tree of the Temple

Sthanikar - Temple trustee

Sthalapuranams - History of sacred centre of shrine

Sudharsana - Weapon of Vishnu

Sura Padma -Name of a demon

Swaras -Musical notes

Swamigal - Saint

Swayambhu - Self-emanating

T

Theertham - Holy water

Thevaram - The sacred hymns of Saivite Saints

Thiruvilayadal Puranam - Compilation of Divine Sport

Thiruneeru - Sacred ash

Thiruvasi -Creascent shaped backdrop

Thoranam - Free-standing gate(a decorative arch)

Thribanga -Triangled pose

U

Ugra - Anger

Uthama Theertham - Name of a sacred tank

V

Vaigai - Name of river

Vaikuntam - Celestial abode of lord Vishnu

Varada - A pose signifying granting of desires

Varalaru - History

Vajrayutha -Thunderbolt, weapon of Indra

Velli Ambalam - Silver Court

Veerasana - Pose signifying courage

Vimanam - The shrine with its tower

Vibuthi - Sacred ash

Vismaya-Wonderment

Y

Yantram – Mascot

Bibliography

English Books:

DEVAKUNJARI Dr. D. - Madurai through the Ages. *Madurai Meenakshi Sundareshwarar Thirukkoil, Madurai-2010.*

GOPINATH RAO.T.A - Elements of Hindu Iconography - 2 Vols. *Motilal Banarsidoss - 1968.*

JAYACHANDRAN A.V. - Madurai Temple Complex, *Publication Division, Madurai Kamaraj University, Madurai - 1985.*

KRISHNA SASTRI.H - South Indian Images of Gods and Goddesses, *Bharathiya Publishing House, Varnasi - 1974.*

SIVARAMAMURTHI.C. - Nataraja in Art, Thought and Literature, *National Museum, New Delhi.*

SAMBASIVA MUDALIAR Rao Bahadur P. Siva Temple Architecture.

SETHURAMAN.N - Histroy of Pandiars.

Tamil Books:

GOVINDASWAMI AIYAR. M - Thirumalai Nayakkar Charithiram - 1922

MANIVANNAN Dr.L - Pottramarai, *A.R.Publication, Madurai - 2010.*

NARASAIYA - Aalavai

PALANIYAPPAN.E - Koil Maanagar, *Madurai Meenakshi Sundareshwarar Koil - 1963*

PANCHANATHAM PILLAI.R. - Sri Meenakshi Sundareshwar Varalaru. *Madurai Meenakshi Sundareswarar Thirukoil 1959.*

RAMASESHAN Dr.R & Valayapettai Ra.KRISHNAN - Arunagirinathar Adichuvattil Thiruppugazh Thalappayanam, *Thiruppugazh Pathippagam, Chennai - 2008.*

SAAMINATHAIYAR Dr.U.Ve - Kumara Gurupara Swamigal Prabanda Thirattu - *Sri Kumara Guruparam Sangam, Srivai Kuntam - 1961.*

SAAMINATHAIYAR Dr.U.Ve - Thiru Aalavayudaiyur Thiruvilayadal Puranam - 1932.

VALAYAPETTAI Ra.KRISHNAN - Chinthai Niraikkum Siva Vadivangal, *Ananda Vikatan Publication - 2009.*

VASUDEVA SASTRI .K - Taala Samudram, *Tanjavur Saraswathi Mahal Library - 1955.*

KUDAVAYIL BALASUBRAMANIAN Dr.- Gopurakkalai Marabhu

SADHASIVA PANDARATHTHAR T.V.- Pandiar Varalaru

SOMALAY - Madurai Maavattam

SOMASUNDRAM PILLAI J.M - Pandiar Peumaatchi

THIRUVENKATA MUDALIAR - Thiru Allavoi Kadavulathu Thiruvilaiyaadal Puranam *(Paranjothi Munivar Eyatriyathu) Eyatramizh Vilakka Achchukootam, Kanchipuram 1885.*

Souvenir

Madurai Thirukkoil Kumbabisheka Malar, *Arulmigu Meenakshi Sundareshwarar Thirukkoil - 1974*

Thirukkoil Nanneeratap Pervizha Sirappu Malar *Arulmighu Meenakshi Sundareshwarar Thirukkoil - 2009*